MIDDLE CHILDHOOD

Practical Tips to Develop Greater Peace (Yours)
and Responsibility (Theirs) for the Parents of
Children Ages 7 through 12

by JAMES HERZ, MSW, MAT

Forward by Dr. JOYCE BROTHERS

Acknowledgements
Cover & Art: Julie H. Gaidis

Published by the
Effred Family Publications
504 Greely Ave.
St. Louis, Missouri 63119-1830

Printed in the
United State of America

Forward

Because of his broad experience as a parent, teacher, and a mental health social worker, James Herz has given all parents, and anyone who works with children, a valuable tool with which to pry open the doors that lead to understanding young minds.

His new book, Middle Childhood, is a reminder that although perfection in parenting may be the goal, it is an elusive one. There are no rigid rules, no strict formulas for the attainment of this impossible dream, partly because we are always dealing with individual needs as well as with unique problems and situations. It is rather like a parent's struggle to treat all children equally, when in reality, they are not equal and both the parent and child know this. One child is younger, one older, one has special talents in one field, one in another field. If a child feels ill on one day, he or she needs special, not equal, care because this is a time for pampering. The realistic, attainable goal is fair treatment and the parent who takes the time to explain why it cannot always be equal will be appreciated and understood.

This gifted author points out the necessity of building a child's esteem, of encouraging independence, allowing the child to make choices while still protecting him from danger. Mr. Herz addresses the issues of learning to handle anger constructively - how both parents and children can learn to "breathe to ten" before allowing rage to erupt. He talks about the bad habit of always putting the blame on others when anything goes wrong and he reminds parents how negotiation and contracts between parent and child can ease many problems.

This book is indeed a journey over the roads that lead to growing up, roads that are inevitably bumpy and filled with potholes. But this author is an excellent and wise guide who, over and over again, shows readers how to find a smooth detour around what might seem like a huge crevice, and, shows that rather than avoiding the crevice, building a bridge over it allows both parent and child to emerge with self-respect.

Part of creating a climate that will lead to growth and better understanding involves better listening. Parents need to learn to listen more attentively to their children and children need equally to be taught to listen and absorb what parents say. Sometimes a dash of humor promotes retention and Mr. Herz is not afraid of using this. The readers who listen to the messages in this book will profit and so will their children.

Dr. Joyce Brothers

Acknowledgments

Foremost, I want to thank my families of origin and of marriage; they have helped me form my ever-improving parenting via example, love, encouragement, experience, and never-ending opportunities to practice humility.

Second, I wish to thank my friends Jerry, Louis, Gary, Carol, Dick, and John for years of friendship as well as my colleagues at Centers for Psychological Growth and at St. Monica School for support (plus cooperating in my various opinion surveys); they have helped me become the person I am through play, study, and work.

Last, I must thank the editors, artists and printers — those paid by check and those paid by pizza — for reviewing this book; they were honest and constructive in their criticism. In specific: Julie Gaidis for her artwork and ability to make written concepts into graphic form on the cover and throughout the text; David Morgan and Susan Sunderman for their honest critiques and editing; and Evonne Weinhuas for the hints and encouragement that only a successful author who has been through the publishing process can fully understand. And, of course, to Dr. Joyce Brothers for having the confidence in my manuscript to write the forward.

Contents

Introduction

The ages of 7 through 12, the years of middle childhood, are special developmental times needing special approaches to parenting. Your children are neither old preschoolers nor young teens. They are in the middle space between two distinct stages with an approach to life with a need for parenting interaction all their own. *Middle Childhood* is written to you, the parent, to help you be more effective in childrearing while being an advocate and for your child's sense of fairness combined with his or her need for appropriate authority. Effective parenting means setting realistic parenting goals, raising children with a balanced commitment to both your family and yourself. Balanced parenting, like all aspects of life, is forever in flux and requires flexibility. *Parenting is an excursion* full of change and surprises which is usually subtle but sometimes glaring, usually smooth, but sometimes chaotic, usually positive and enjoyable but sometimes unwanted, undeserved, and uncomfortable. Balance requires love, mutual respect, and teamwork — none of which are easy to maintain. And parenting during the middle childhood years requires the use of practical techniques so that love, mutual respect, self-esteem for all – and for your sanity – remain intact over these years.

Remember that *most* of what we do to encourage, motivate, discipline, and love our children works *most* of the time. Use the practical tips and information in these chapters to make yourself more resourceful. Make *small* changes in your style when needed. Eventually, you will see *big* results.

Middle Childhood is arranged into six sections each consisting of several chapters. The first is "Getting Started" which covers the factors of healthy versus dysfunctional families (with the understanding that all families are neither perfect nor totally flawed), tips on how to evaluate your relationships with your children, how to stay calm in the face of frustration, and how to spot your personal strengths and weaknesses in parenting. The next section, "The Normals" examines a fictitious family and the highs and lows of the parents and their middle childhood children. Section three, "Mental Health Problems," explains special emotional problems children can develop including over-anxiety, depression, attention deficit hyperactivity disorder (which is more a condition of attributes and liabilities than a problem-laden disorder), and learning disabilities as these syndromes effect family life. Section four, "Caroline and the Counselor," examines a composite, but not actual, family in therapy with their middle-childhood daughter. The fifth section explains the specifics of development for each age of the middle childhood years detailing what is normal, what is problematic, and how to keep your composure by being able to state (as my wife once exclaimed to one of our children as he ran through the house), "Stop acting your age!" The final section, "Discipline and Interventions" covers activities which work best in middle childhood, considering a child's age together with the specific problems discussed in section three, with references to healthy family life as described in section one, and using the lessons learned through the examples of The Normals and Caroline. Each chapter contains an italicized segue bridging the previous chapter to the next and a summary to add hints or special considerations at the close of each chapter.

As to gender, the chapters are written alternatively using the pronouns he and she. This avoids the cumbersome "he/she" or using only the word "he." Further, this supports my belief that both fathers and mothers must strive to improve their parenting skills.

The names, ages, sex, and specific predicaments of all people mentioned in this book have been altered to protect confidentially and anonymity. Actual families were not used even in part, except in some of the chapters were I, usually with some egg on my face, describe personal predicaments.

Last, the middle childhood years, although fraught with feelings of confusion by children and times of exasperation by parents, is a period mostly full of enthusiasm for living and great growth in every aspect of life for all. Take the opportunity to enjoy your children whenever you can. They will enjoy and respect you more in return.

SECTION 1
GETTING STARTED

The eleven chapters in this section explain how healthier families share love and trust as well as avoid overreactions by keeping emotions and expectations in perspective. Equally, the chapters on codependency, the term for relationships in which there is more dysfunction than health, explain how breakdowns in trust and accountability contagiously spread emotional and social illness throughout the home.

I use the phrase "healthier families" because the best of families have their deficits while the least sound of families also have their share of assets. As stated in the introduction, most of our parenting techniques work most of the time with most of our children. However, often we know less about our emotions and motives than we think we do. By the end of this section, you will know more. And the more we know about ourselves, the higher our self-awareness of why we do what we do, which results in improved and the more practical our parenting decisions and self-control.

Most of us turn to parenting resources —friends, relatives, books, professionals, internet support lines, and so on — when "what works most of the time" is not working. Breathing to ten is the first step in preventing parental overreaction while we decide whether or how to intervene with the problem, to ignore it, or merely to wait while observing from a safe distance.

Chapter 1: Breathing To Ten

Sending your child to Siberia for a month without food or phone is abuse. *Wanting to do it* at times is normal. Learning to effectively breathe to ten allows you to regain your composure, your parenting sense of balance. Here are the basic guidelines:

1. Breathe slowly and deeply. *Emphasis here is on the word slowly.* Feel your diaphragm move in and out. When we are tense, we tend to breathe rapidly and with our chest muscles. The result, unfortunately, is to take even quicker, shorter breaths while increasing the tension in the chest instead of relaxing. We get caught in an emotional and physical negative cycle.

2. Let your shoulders and hands hang loose. Unclench your teeth. Slow breathing rather than counting is the key to attaining and maintaining calm.

3. Practice this breathing a few times daily for one minute each time. Practice in traffic. Practice when you hear thunder. Practice while you pay bills. After you practice for a couple of days, try

breathing to ten while envisioning your most frustrating situations.

4. Once you are adept at relaxing while imagining stressful predicaments, teach the others in your household to breathe to ten. If you and your child can take deep breaths in the midst of battle, everyone's feelings are less likely to get hurt. Disagreements that turn to ugly, insulting, and one-sided parent victories encourage resentment if not revenge by your child. Breathing to ten encourages respect by both of you *even if you are the only one using it.* Since you are at least modeling self-discipline by establishing your own sense of calm, there is less chance of continuing or escalating the conflict.

5. When you sense an argument intensifying, take these additional steps while you breathe: (a) Put your hands in your pockets or lock your hands behind your back. This action cuts down angry gestures and makes intimidation or physical violence by you less possible; (b) Take two steps backward. When tempers are rising, the other person becomes an opponent instead of a loved one. And when that opponent is only a few menacing inches away, he fills your entire view, thus throwing your perspective of the the immediate situation out of its actual importance.

These steps backward help reset your visual sense of what is actually taking place. Of course, this works best when both of you move back simultaneously, but do not wait for the other person to move first.

*****

Many years ago, a nine-year-old client proudly told me that she had become furious at her brother but had calmly breathed to ten *before she slugged him.* I realized then that I'd placed too much emphasis on the counting part. When we are under stress our emotional responses are close to a nine-year old's level. By breathing to ten we can let our adult understanding and self-control take over again.

I rushed upstairs one evening after just returning home after a long, hectic workday. While breathing to ten, I sat on my son's bed and found myself overcome with a love and a spiritual warmth impossible to express in words. At such times I feel prosperous and secure regardless of my credit card balances. We all need to feel accepted and loved by others. We have a need to give love as well as to accept it.

Acceptance And Love

Jeffery, my new eleven-year-old client, and I were just getting to know each other. We had just walked into my office, leaving his parents behind in the waiting room. I asked him what game on my shelf he wanted to play, but he did not respond. I encouraged him to pick any one. He just sat there, limp.

"When you were in the waiting room you were excited and said you could not wait to play with the toys I have. What made you lose your enthusiasm, Jeff?"

"I still want to play," he said softly. "But I don't know which one I'm *supposed* to pick."

"Jeffrey, do you sometimes feel that you have to figure out what other people want so they will like you? And, when you feel that way do you even know what it is that you want for yourself?"

"Sometimes that happens with my mom and dad. I think they like me best when I tell them about school. They get bored when I tell them about playing in the creek with my friends."

Jeffrey felt that his parents were not accepting the whole Jeffrey, but just the parts of him that were of greatest interest to them even though their concerns were well-meant — to plan for his educational and professional future — their attention to him was conditional and he responded with caution and anxiety. Conditional love is affection and attention with strings attached. It is not the full parental acceptance of the whole child as a person with both strengths and weaknesses. When attention to our children is predicated on rules and conditions, *and this pattern is ongoing,* family breakdown results. We all require the fabric of a lovable identity for weaving healthy self-esteem and as the basis for self-acceptance. Love, without condition, is the requirement to be able to succeed without conceit, to fail with humility, and view others without prejudice. Sometimes, as adults, we over-focus on adult-level concerns and, as an unplanned result, we neglect the childhood building blocks necessary to become the self-assured adults we want to our children to be. (This building-block theme will be covered in depth in the section on middle childhood development.) When we are raised with the jewels of acceptance and love, we pass them on to our children. If we did not have these jewels as children ourselves, it is difficult to share them in our family when we are parents.

I called Jeffrey's parents in from the waiting room and explained Jeffery's insecurities to them. Four sessions later, Jeffery's anxieties had been significantly relieved and therapy was concluded. We had cake for Jeffery's graduation — a ceremony for his parents' effort and courage as well as for his.

*****

There is limited time and, as we age, a limit to our energy to accomplish all our vocational, social, and recreational goals. Strive to find more ways to share these aspects of your life with your children. *Make small changes* in how you spend your hours *now*. Major changes in lifestyle seldom last very long. Your children will benefit immensely in the long run from your alterations. So will their children.And their children. And so will you.

Love, acceptance, and teaching our children by doing various activities with them are the basics of healthier families. Adults who model teamwork, mutual respect, and time for personal interests and goals are also basics for family health and marital satisfaction. The balancing of parenting, marriage, and individual commitments is an everlasting yet unavoidable task to be tackled on an ongoing basis. As a reminder, however, this task, for the most part, is a highly rewarding and enjoyable one.

Healthy Families

Families are living systems that change over time.They develop like the people in them. We do not just become adults and then not mature any more. Families are groups having social and organizational interdependency needs. Like a well-run office, leaders (parents) are needed but *autocratic bosses are disliked* and avoided. Workers (children) follow office rules, take some sick days when they are physically unhealthy or emotionally in need of a break, and use tact and respect in voicing their complaints about policies ("Why do I always have to do the dishes!"). And, to continue this analogy, the older teens and college students would be the middle managers.

Families are, simultaneously, also a mixture of individuals, each having his or her own needs and goals. Each person, regardless of age, has unique feelings, reactions, preferences, favorite pizza toppings, and ice cream flavors. No wonder Baskin-Robbins and Pizza Hut are always so busy. In families, both the requirements of the individual and the group coexist at all times such that these two parts of the family *naturally come into conflict and cooperation* on a regular basis. The healthy family system is flexible enough to adapt when necessary as the members mature — a process that is never ending on both personal and group levels. This ongoing process of growth and change, coping with the normal conflicts, results in stronger group bonds and higher individual esteem. In the healthier family, there is an ongoing striving for balance between personal and group issues. College savings, buying the son or daughter a needed scout uniform, getting braces, and making summer plans, can be forces eating away at limited finances all at one time. Balance for the time may include chores, playing with friends, parents' night out, helping the kids with homework, staying in shape: twenty-nine hours worth of activity squeezed into sixteen waking hours.

The issue of conflict becomes a matter of identity and personal boundaries surrounding any given topic. Boundaries are the communication lines of openness and defense that define who else can "come in" and "stay out" of any person's thoughts, feelings, and physical self. Like a child's bedroom, sometimes she is comfortable with others entering and sometimes she wants privacy — the same is true of the parents' bedroom. Sometimes the child is willing to talk openly, frankly, about a personal subject and other times not, depending upon the trust and acceptance the child feels her listener has for her. Revealing about personal issues, the opening of one's boundaries, occurs more frequently when trust and respect are perceived.

In human development, there are loose boundaries between parent and child at infancy. The parent makes all decisions when the child is more dependent in the relationship. The adult has an identity as a unique being while the infant does not. The infant's increasing skills in crying, cooing, and smiling make her more of an active participant with her social environment. As she continues to develop toward adulthood, forming a more solid and consistent identity of herself, she will normally create increasingly firm boundaries around herself that are relaxed only in an environment of perceived trust.

Where conditional love is present, there is less trust in general. A suspicious person does not let others fully enter her emotional room. When the mutual trust needed to open boundaries is not present, codependency, the relationship symptom of dysfunctional families, exists. Codependency will be discussed in the next chapter.

*****

All families and all individuals have moments of great insight, compassion, loyalty, and self-control. We also all have moments of panic, invasion, and memories of injurious comments we wish had never been uttered by us or to us. As a model for our children, appropriately for their age, we need to share some of our stronger and weaker moments with them. Regarding our personal boundaries, we seldom tell every detail of our history to any one person. Some items we choose to keep in our mental lockbox. The upcoming section on mental health problems will help you differentiate between the time when keeping personal items is a mere right to privacy as opposed to a signal that emotional concerns exist. This differentiation will be explained in the forthcoming chapter about keeping secrets.

Authority of parents over their children and division of labor are necessary in all families. Family health versus emotional illness occurs when decisions are repeatedly made arbitrarily by a parent (or the parents together) or when children are continually manipulated or coerced into compliance. Health versus dysfunction is a matter of degree, intensity, and frequency since there certainly are times when parents must be absolute in enforcing rules. The parent decides and dictates, for example, when the child requires medical attention, attends school, or acts disrespectfully to others in situations where she may not responsible enough, is unable, or is too immature or impaired in some way to do what is really necessary, and appropriate. Look at how you reach your decision more than at what actual decision is reached. Health and dysfunction are based on the process of how we run our families more than what our family actually does.

Codependency: Dysfunctional Family Patterns

Codependency exists when at least one person in a relationship does not respect healthy family boundaries and mutual respect as explained in the previous chapter. A codependent person is one who tends to unnecessarily relinquish control over his own boundaries (unnecessary passivity) *or* tends to dominate others' boundaries when not appropriate (unnecessary aggression). Codependency exists when our self-control is inflexible and results in ongoing use of coercion or feigned helplessness in response to asserting ourselves in the face of stress or necessary compromise. It is termed *codependency* as the individual views his moods and behavior as dependent on what others do. The codependent person does not act assertively in the healthy two-part family system although he may understand it cognitively. He sees only one part of the group such that he denies his own individuality *or* insists that he is the ruler of the family. Similar to not conforming to a healthy lifestyle of diet and exercise, in relationships we may understand what to do but overreact in the midst of stress. It is as if we have learned about swimming by practicing only on the dock: once we enter the water, a whole new situation is suddenly upon us. Often, this dictator position may be assumed for the best of reasons. However, the healthy process of teamwork with spouses and children breaks down as a result. A codependent, in short, is likely to allow others to tell him what to do or insist that others follow his demands. In terms of parenting, if your ten-year-old's "friend" wants your son to steal from a store, it is certainly your obligation to limit that friendship. Restricting your son's social activity is necessary to protect your family from unhealthy outside influences just as you would not allow polluted drinking water to knowingly come into your home. However, if you limit your son's friendships merely because you do not approve of the friend's parents' political or religious views, that is a codependent abuse of your parental authority. (Of course, you would explain to your son why you feel the opposing views are different from yours, but that is far different from making your son drop the friend he has chosen.) Drug and vandalism problems certainly do require your intervention as well.

The goal of emotional health is, again, a balancing act between accepting *what you can versus cannot control* and then taking responsible action. We cannot control other people, at least, not in the long run. Codependents "win" numerous battles and "avoid" various discomforts but regularly lose the ongoing respect and trust necessary for peaceful compromise and enduring love. We are responsible for our own actions and for making plans so that problems do not recur. Further, we have a responsibility to fairness, caring, and commiseration to ourselves and to one another. Insisting that your daughter, aged eight, use certain crayons to color a picture of her TV heroine is codependent. Insisting that she get her homework done is healthy parenting.

Aggressive and passive codependents tend to choose each other for dating and marriage under the assumption that they have created a complementary relationship. Unfortunately, once their honeymoon period wanes, one or both partners lose satisfaction with the arrangement as there is little trust, low mutual respect, conditional love, and inflexibility in coping with conflict. Subtle or open power battles begin as a result.

In most codependent marriages, *the children become the parents' battleground* since healthy conflict resolution is less possible for the parents as a couple. Thus, Mom says "no" to having more ice cream while Dad counters with, "Sure, Honey, Mom's just fussy," (The underlying message in Dad's comment is that he loves the daughter best and mom is irrational via her moodiness.) The parents may switch Mom-as-restrictive and Dad-as-generous roles at any time. *Middle Childhood* will help you become more successful in your part of raising healthy children.

*****

Codependency is not a set-in-stone condition, but a *pattern* of unnecessary control and unrealistic fear of catastrophe if control is diminished or not exercised. To the contrary, the more that power to make decisions is shared, the more that control is eventually gained and lasting respect received by *all in the family*. Considering the shifting ability of children to make decisions according to their age, see the section on development when you are unsure about what to do. As a parent, I know that feeling unsure is a regular occurrence. I often remind myself it is also a natural occurrence.

A secondary aspect of the codependent pattern is the tendency to either panic or underreact to the actual seriousness of a problem or situation. Again, since all of us have moments of overreaction, here is a personal example of a predicament in which my desire for perfection ran in to a wall called reality.

Emergencies & Buttons

One ominously gray morning a number of years ago, I was preparing to drive my oldest son to school (including the neighbors in our carpool) and then get my youngest son to daycare. Unfortunately, Rob, aged four, had a tantrum scheduled for the same time. I *had* to get the kids to school before the bell. I also *had* to keep Rob from screeching and holding us up. I *had* to have my preschooler looking happy and cheerful by the time we arrived at daycare. And I *had* to get to work on time looking calm myself. Since I'm the expert on children, there was no chance that I, Mr. Counselor, would ever fall victim to being a perfectionist with my own progeny. Right.

With all the "had to's", there was an emergency brewing. And in emergencies, like anyone else who is not trained in emergency work, I overreacted. Rob got spanked and yelled at. The kids got to school a bit late. And I remained annoyed at my youngest (who had the audacity to act his age when I did not want him to) well into my second cup of decaf. There would be no need for regular coffee this morning: my blood pressure was already up.

As with many *apparent* emergencies, this had not really been an emergency at all. Emergency thinking is a form of panic. It occurs when one or more of our buttons is being pushed. Buttons are large emotional targets we all have that a blindfolded chicken can hit from fifty yards away. For example, one of my buttons is a fear that certain others my make issue of my short stature. When under stress, that button gets very sensitive. My baldness is not a button for me, though some bald men wear their target on top of their heads like bad toupees. (This does not mean you shouldn't try some Rogaine to help soothe a bit of vanity. Looking our best is a sign of esteem as long as we do not obsess or become compulsive about it.) A friend of mine hates his nose, and under pressure in public, all of his positive qualities become dwarfed by the nose's shadow.

The positive converse of buttons are "warm spots." These are the past experiences that evoke our smiles and inner warmth when we remember them. In the healthier families, the individuals have a balance such that there are more warm spots than buttons for the individuals as well as for the family unit. Further, warm spot feelings of pride and joy last longer than the anger and fear which accompany our targets of terror — strive to achieve this balance if it does not already exist for you. We all have buttons that symbolize our insecurities. On that particular dreary morning, a button was being pushed from hundreds of miles away, over thirty years ago, saying that tardiness is a sin and a sign of failure. Certainly, punctuality is important, but being late sometimes is not a signal for terror.

Once I regained my composure, I made a plan to handle future carpool tantrums differently and, hopefully, more effectively. I did not know for sure if my revised procedure would work better until another surprise test showed up, although I did run my ideas past a colleague or two. And I firmly told the buttons to leave me alone.

Do not confuse and mix your buttons with true emergencies any more than possible. Breathe to ten instead.

*****

14

The healthier families have irrational behaviors and emotional upheavals from time to time. The more dysfunctional families, however, do not emerge from the aftermath with a clear view of the incident — including the courage to say, "Ok, so we're not perfect," a plan to avoid reoccurrences, and the humility to admit mistakes to others. In sharing our foibles with friends, we usually get support and often a few good laughs as well.

Feeling unhappy with ourselves is appropriate after parenting upheavals. Without such emotional discomfort we would not seek more effective solutions and means to prevent reoccurrences. My story of Rob and the "carpool disaster" continues.

Good Guilt — Bad Guilt

I should have seen it coming, It was sure to be "one of those days." And, as you just read, it certainly started out that way. Looking back, I had hints of Rob's inevitable tantrum. The rush of schoolday-workday mornings can be like that. We had run out of Rob's favorite cereal. It was drizzling outside and his favorite umbrella was nowhere to be found. He had reached his young breaking point. His tantrum, combined with my escalating buttons, created *my* breaking point.

On the mutually silent drive to daycare, little Rob apologized. His eyes were red with the remnants of tears. I apologized, too. The rest of my day was not "one of those days," but I had a somber commute to the office filled with guilt about the morning struggle. Although our battle was an incident that happens in the healthiest of households. *Rob had* acted his age. I had not. I was not going to place all the blame on him. My emotions, combined with some bad luck, were the basis of the problem.

As the day continued, I had to decide if the incident was to result in good guilt or bad guilt for me. *Bad guilt* is the kind that we use to belittle and berate ourselves. It is the inner voice we use to keep telling ourselves we are failures as persons — the same overreactive voice that creates and lubricates our buttons. I could have spent the day telling myself, "I'm such a bully to my son. He will never love me because of what happened today. More proof of what a lousy parent I am."

Good guilt is the kind of emotional discomfort we use as a healthy incentive to avoid doing a certain something again. For example, "I feel bad about this morning. Next time I will try to reset my priorities to focus on keeping calm. Being a healthy parent means this particular screw-up will not happen again."

I put stationery in the car glove compartment for writing tardy-to-school notes along with earplugs to muffle the tantrum shrieks. I realize that the earplugs may not be ideal for traffic safety, but are better for my sanity as well as for driver concentration. As another option, commonly called bribery, I put a box of animal crackers in the glove box, too. And, if the bribery did not work to stop Rob's screeching, at least I could eat them to soothe myself.

Good guilt is good for all involved. Bad guilt is the opposite. Good guilt models the responsibility and esteem we have in ourselves. The modeling of our successes and our failures continues to be the best teacher of humility and self-acceptance there is. If we tend to get mired in the self-humiliation of bad guilt, our children will do the same to themselves and, eventually, to their children.

*****

After assessing our guilt and licking our wounded feelings, we may decide that our actions were correct and that we would repeat them in similar situations. The purpose of guilt is to force an honest assessment. Often we will require a more objective consultation including a talk with a friend or relative who will provide a more candid opinion in contrast to our subjective viewpoint.

As to those schoolday-workday mornings...if you can get everyone out on time, with everyone having some form of nourishment, with clothing and shoes on, and lunches or meal money in hand, you have gotten off to a fine start! Any additional moments you can get with the paper, TV, books, coffee or tea for yourself, is a bonus.

Anger is like other emotions we have discussed: love, frustration, panic, peace, stress, and confusion. All feelings have their times and places for both appropriate expression and where postponement is the better course of action. There are situations calling for candid venting and situations calling for diplomatic restraint. The feelings themselves pop up on their own and each of us is more prone to experiencing some emotions more than others. There are no wrong emotions. The key is learning when to openly express or withhold each option. My hint, per usual, is to avoid attempting perfection. Try your honest-to-yourself-best to aim for improvement. When in doubt: breathe.

Anger: Helpful & Hurtful

Too many people are raised with a fear of anger (not violence, per se, although that is sometimes inappropriately implied as intimidation.) Letting someone else get angry or expressing your own anger *fairly* will not hurt you, although it certainly feels better to be at the expressing end of the fury than to be at the receiving end. *Being at the receiving end of temper is uncomfortable* but not dangerous. In fact, your relationships in general are in less danger in the long run when healthy anger is allowed and encouraged by your model. In healthy anger, the emphasis is on the concept of fairness. Fairness can be defined as taking responsibility for your own behavior, feelings, and statements without blaming the other person as the cause for your eruption. Specifically, fairness in the expression of anger means staying on the subject and not digressing into attacking the other person's character. Anger full of blame is unhealthy because the goal is then to intimidate and control others.

Angry blame is not truly expression of a feeling but rather manipulation. Angry blame is a form of verbal abuse when it continues.

One way to tell healthy anger from blaming anger is whether the eventual *goal is to seek a mutually agreed upon solution.* Keep track of the outcomes of your arguments to assess what your real intent may have been. Get to know your patterns and honestly acknowledge them. As I did following my carpool disaster morning, acknowledge your interpersonal liabilities and then humbly take steps toward improvement.

When someone reveals healthy anger to you, *breathe* and listen. Hearing the other person's view does not mean you are agreeing. Try to stay calm and attempt to understand the expressor's point of view. Equally, just because the expressor is annoyed does not mean his or her observations are inaccurate. An angry person is equally as correct as a passive one.

The fear of danger comes from two possible sources. First, when others (usually our parents) got angry, intense discomfort usually ensued via punishment or embarrassment. Thus, discomfort in some form was either immediate or coming in the near future. Second, when you are a child, your parents may not have let you express your anger in any form. You may have been ridiculed as being overly emotional or immature or they may have punished you for losing your temper. The message in your parents' behavior in such scenarios said, "I do not want to hear your displeasures about me as a parent." Their fear of anger button would become your button, too.

Unexpressed anger is not healthy. Emotions — and anger is an emotion - are like long balloons. When you squeeze one end, the air just goes to the other end. Anger, like the air in the balloon, does not disappear, but causes subsequent and greater trouble manifesting in stress, medical problems, accidents, divorce, resentful children, overeating, anxiety, low esteem, and/or depression. This is true for ongoing repression of any specific emotion.

Returning to venting anger fairly, vent at the person with whom you are upset. Stay on the topic as best as you can. Breathe to ten when you feel a sense of needing to win your point as opposed to explaining the basis for your displeasure. If you find you are getting out of control, that you are becoming desperate to gain an immediate victory, disengage. Back off. Disengaging requires you to leave the room until you can talk rationally. Equally, when the receiver disengages from the argument, allow him his distance to lower his hurt or rising responsive temper. Allow others to vent honestly to you and your relationships with your spouse and children *will* be healthier.

*****

Of course, if you are inconsistent about your expressions and receptions of anger, others will not feel trusting about communicating annoyances with you. Consistency is a key factor. As a reminder to avoid perfectionism, consistency can be defined as doing what you say you will at least three-quarters of the time. The main goal is to avoid repetition of the misuse of anger. And as the appropriate timing and fair expression of anger replaces the manipulative and power-based abuse, mutual self-respect and trust will increase in your home as fear and distrust eventually decrease.

Remember — venting anger does not necessarily mean yelling and gnashing your teeth. The calmer you are in your expression, the calmer your listener will stay as well.

Now that you are becoming more effective in your parenting via dealing more smoothly with emotions, lessening perfectionism, improving practicality, keeping calmer, and using guilt and anger more healthfully you will be minimizing the patterns that increase family dysfunction at the same time. The children in middle childhood will certainly challenge you in subtle and not-so-subtle ways. You, like me, will be prepared for some of these challenges while others will catch you unaware. About Me Books are your personal lists of when you are most and least efficient as a parent. These notebooks help prevent pitfalls and increase successes. Such record keeping helps us start situations anew with the aid of the lessons learned from our parenting experience and personal history.

About Me Books

About Me Books are special diaries of where and when we are at our best and when we are most vulnerable to failure. For *Middle Childhood* we are focusing on parenting, although this diary is effective with any situation we have encountered and might encounter again. About Me Books are simple, organized lists of our better and lesser parenting moments: what caused the failures and what influenced the successes. It is best to keep this project simple since complex projects seldom get completed or done with regularity.

Step One: Get a spiral notebook. Pick the color and style you like best and decorate it if you care to. Hey, parenting is supposed to mostly enjoyable. Get out your crayons and markers and go to it.

Step Two: Have the first page be your table of contents

for the various aspects of family life. Topics might include; times for discussions, discipline for my youngest child, discipline for my middle child, discipline for my oldest child, my emotional buttons, parenting advice given by my parents, people to call when the kids are driving me crazy, rewards for my youngest child, rewards for my middle child, rewards for my oldest child, and so on. Did I mention *people to call when the kids are driving me crazy?*

Step Three: As you turn the pages, you will always have a right-hand page and left-hand page facing you with the spiral binding in the center. Both pages are used for the same subject. The left page facing you is for the *positive* items of the subject and the right page for the *negative* aspects. For example, I'd have a section for "workday-schoolday mornings" since these are touchy times for me. (You, for example may find mornings easy but have more ups and downs with your children's bedtimes.) On the left (positive) page I would list (1) earplugs for noise muffling, (2) animal crackers, and (3) notepad for tardy notes. A few days later, I might add (4) keep Doobie Brothers tape in car, and, a week later add, (5) make a tape with friends and my wife all telling me, "Stay calm, you can do it." Add ideas as they come up. On the negative side for these mornings, I would list the problems to avoid such as (1) running out of Fruit Loops and (2) buttons about having to be exactly on time as a basis for my self-esteem. A few days later I might add (3) keep a bag of Fruit Loops in the back seat for emergency use and (here's a tough one for a non morning person like me) (4) get up ten minutes earlier so there is time to disengage and keep my temper cool if needed. That way I can be on time daily, which is important. On a morning that looks like it is going downhill fast, I can grab my About Me Book and quickly review what to do and what not to do. Then I can decide what I can and cannot change about that particular morning.

Write the items as a list, not as long descriptions. The

memory of the incident will be a sufficient narrative. Situations that are emotionally charged will not be forgotten. What you will have is a quick-reference guide to gloss over while taking your deep breaths. As to the part of luck, remember that for every morning that there *is not* a car stuck in your lane of the highway, good luck has occurred. *Luck flows both ways* so do not focus solely on the adverse occasions. Keeping track of your warm spots is a great way to reset a bleak outlook.

*****

Possibly the most important topic area I have in my About Me Book is "consultants." I have separate lists for parenting consultants, marriage consultants, and business consultants. For each of these topics I have a list of who has given helpful advice and whose hints have not been particularly helpful. Certain friends make the positive page for business but not for marriage. Others are on top of the parenting sheet but not the business one. Our most effective consultants, however, are the ones who constructively yet delicately will tell us what we *need to hear* over what we might *prefer to hear.*

In her introduction to Middle Childhood, Dr. Brothers mentioned that humor can often be a useful tension reliever. Laughing and chuckling can undoubtedly have a salubrious effect, soothing our hurt feelings when given with love, and making life more enjoyable when given in the appropriate doses and the timing is right. Snorts, snickers, and snide smirks are seldom signs of respectful humor.

What's Funny? What Isn't?

Although there are common themes in what makes us chuckle, the question in the title above is really impossible to answer. Personal preferences, as well as individual sore spots, effect what we feel is humorous or is not. I knew some jokes that would receive peals of laughter in the high school boys' locker room. The same comments would have gotten me tarred and feathered if I'd told it to a group of girls.

One summer, in the community pool shower room, I saw a boy about ten put his right hand under his left arm pit to produce a sound very similar to that of a human passing gas. He and his buddy were in hysterics. Another father and I were humored by the boys' joy in reproducing body sounds. What was humorous to us parents was far different from what the kids were enjoying regarding their antics.

A past colleague of mine had a speech deficit that was barely noticeable. However, there was a certain unmentionable expletive that she never could quite pronounce distinctly. Some people in the office teased her about this, while others offered her synonyms to use as alternatives although those words did not carry quite the same spirit or emphasis that the original term did. When mocked or imitated by friends she usually traded insults with us and we all laughed. Sometimes, however, she admitted that she felt embarrassed or angry when strangers would call attention to her errors.

Humor is individually appreciated based upon the audience, for example, men vs women, age (kids versus adults), position (authority versus student or employee), situation (public or private), and our view of the humorist (friend or foe). The matter of personal taste in slapstick, satire, or puns is not of issue since these are merely styles of humor. Be sensitive to how, where, and *what* you joke about. Be aware of your buttons when you are the receiver. Be especially aware of your intentions when you are the comedian. Was your joke meant to entertain, share, educate, embarrass, soothe, compete, or insult? As a model to your children in sharing respect for yourself and others, do not repeat hurtful quips no matter how innocent or harmless you felt your comment was. Humor is in the ears of the beholder.

*****

Most humor is fun for everyone involved. However, we all tell jokes that we may later realize were inappropriate or hurtful. Sometimes someone else helps us realize our error on the spot. Sometimes they do this with a retort, a friendly jab, a serious educational tone, or with a vengeful attack. Breathe to ten when this happens. Be sensitive. Be respectful. Use your About Me Book when you sense a pattern of problems. Most of all, *laugh when you can.*

This chapter is a variation on the topics of the buttons and non-emergencies that we are subject to in parenthood. Most of us have certain aspects of our own childhoods we wish we could do over. As result we press our children to be better students, to try harder in art, to be a scout — whatever we wanted to do but did not and tried but failed at, wanted to have but could not get, and so on. Our job as parents most certainly includes helping our children be successful at a number of activities as well as protect them from various forms of failure and injury. Sometimes our past miseries become buttons and our response is to overcontrol our children's interests and activities thereby, sadly, not listening effectively to what goals and interests they have.

Be aware that doing something over in life may not make a positive difference, but merely a difference. Your present situation may be worse if you had taken a different path. Yes, it may be better also, but the truth is, we will never really know. (This comment, however, seldom applies to past tragedies and traumas we may have suffered.) But, in general, we need to accept what choices we have made, learn from them, and move on emotionally. Our children will also benefit when we can do this.

Sports For Young And Old Alike

I coached my son's soccer team in second, third, and fourth grades. For the most part, I had as much enjoyment the year they tied one game — their best scoring display of the season — as I had the year their only loss was a forfeit because we had gone to the wrong field. Okay, *it was more fun* the winning year, but my pride, and the team's, did not show a tremendous difference. My policy was to assign each parent a night to come and assist during practice which, in some cases, meant keeping the kids out of the creek. We really did create a team effort. These early grades were deemed instructional years by the league. The emphasis was on learning basic skills, teamwork, and sportsmanship. The emphasis was *not on* winning. The strongest and weakest athletes played the same amount of time. This was definitely not the World Cup or the Olympics.

I remember one father staying after a game, angrily kicking a ball to his son, telling the youngster that only practice would prevent his blatant errors from occurring in future games. The child was embarrassed and hurt. No words of encouragement from his coaches could soothe the wounds of humiliation from Dad. There was nothing I could do to mend their mutual shame about the boy's imperfect play. Dad clearly did not accept his son playing at his age level. The father expected his son to play well beyond his age.

Sports, like any other aspect of life, can lend itself to togetherness, growth, pride, and learning all about humility. But like all other aspects too, there are boundaries involved. When your child's performance on the field reflects your esteem, follow what you have learned so far:

1. Breathe to ten when the subject of practice arises.

2. Set a new goal for your behavior and attitude.

3. Make an entry in your About Me Book.

4. Listen to your child's view as she sees it. If the child holds "bad guilt" (shame), explain your feelings to her — you build mutual respect through sharing your dreams and fears.

5. Check your own childhood buttons. Why is your child's performance your issue? Remember that easing your shame *is your responsibility* — your

child cannot do this for you vicariously.

6. Review your own definitions of success as a parent to find what is off balance for you.

Ideally, sports should be mostly for fun, fitness, and socializing. The competition is clear enough even when we do not emphasize it. Admittedly, it is more enjoyable to win than to lose, but in the right atmosphere, it does not make much difference — certainly not to the kids.

*****

"If only _____ had happened...things would be better now." "If only I had _____ instead of _____." " If only _____ had loved me more." Fill in the blanks any way you want. If we obsess upon these "if onlys" we impede our personal growth and the accompanying maturity of our children. The peace and responsibility goals of this book are based greatly upon our own maturity and humility. Humility stings a bit — a lot like the season our team was winless. But the pride of the players and parents was high. And we celebrated with our cookies, cake, and soda party right after our last game — just as we did every year.

Last in this section of basics for healthy parenting is a lesson I seem to keep relearning again and again. (I know that sentence was redundant, but this point is a biggie.) Our children grow so quickly — take advantage of the available time with them. My father said recently, when I asked what wisdom he wanted passed on to his children and grandchildren, "Having a job that is meaningful and a solid income are important, but making money isn't all it's cracked up to be. Be sure to take time for your children, your spouse, and yourself."

"Trivialities": A Play With A Moral

Act 1, scene 1. *The bathroom. Getting near bedtime.*

Mom, age 37: The tub is full, so please get in. It's been a long day and Mommy's got a headache.

Barbara, age 4: I want bubbles.

Mom: We are out of bubbles, honey. Dad didn't buy a new box yet. (Sure, blame Dad... [Oh, I just know I'll get some juicy letters regarding that comment.]) [Barbara is in tears, heartbroken. Acts as if not having bubbles is a tragedy. *To her it is a tragedy.*]

Mom: [Not feeling sympathy. Only wants to pay the bills and get herself to bed soon.] It's trivial, dear. Just get in and I'll buy some bubble bath tomorrow.

Barbara: [Eyes suddenly sparkle.] We can use some of the pink soap for dishes. That makes lots of bubbles!

Mom: [Heavy sigh.] Okay.

Act 2, final scene. *The bathroom.* Barbara's head is barely visible above bubbles. 15 minutes later on the clock, however, emotional light years have passed.

Barbara: [With gusto.] Hey, Mom, I made a bubble

mountain!

Mom: [Leaning over side of tub, smiling.] Here comes a snow lion to eat the bubble mountain!

[Barbara kicks and giggles. Snow mountain explodes. Bubbles fill the air and a bubble war ensues. Both sides claim victory. *Both won.*]

*****

Moral : Undoubtedly, paying the bills, returning phone calls, and various other mediating priorities exist that our children cannot understand until they are parents themselves. But beware of these excuses becoming too frequent. In this case, I believe the triviality was more Mom's than Barbara's. When feeling unduly rushed, count to ten to turn off your buttons and to slow the anti-perspective clock in your head. *Nature sets few time limits —people set too many.*

SECTION 2:

THE NORMALS — A FAMILY LIKE YOURS & MINE

The Normals, two parents and three children, are a family that tries to be as healthy as possible. In the first section, "Getting Started," the emphasis was on awareness of your own parenting style, communication, and how to make realistic improvements. The Normals are forever trying to do the same thing both as individual parents and as a parenting team. The Normals are a fictional family created to show how the lessons covered in "Getting Started" actually look in action. The children span the years of middle childhood. The parents are your age.

We all have our emergency buttons. Although we may hate to admit it, our children usually know exactly where these buttons are and often aim directly for them. We call this "manipulating one's parents" or, more commonly, "getting to us again." Sometimes we ignore these direct hits, sometimes we respond smoothly, sometimes we surprise them with a reaction they had not considered, and sometimes we thoroughly overreact. Sometimes our children hit our sore spots on "one of those days" either by design or by innocence. The former we call "bad timing" and the latter we call "bad luck." Welcome, children and parents, to the human race.

Meet The Normals: A Fictional Family

The Normal family consists of two parents, Hal and Sal, two daughters, Cindy, 12, Mindy, 10, and son, Joey, 7. They live in a neighborhood a lot like yours. For the most part, they are a happy family. They all usually help clean the house with a minimum of whining. They all take their turns feeding and walking the dog, although some need more reminders than others. And they all like the same pizza topping: mushrooms. I told you this is fiction.

Cindy and Mindy usually play well together although they have the usual arguments over rules, cheating, and fairness. Sometimes their arguments approach battle proportions, which Hal despises. At these times, Hal feels as if a civil defense whistle is blowing in his ear while he has a migraine. Thus, when the girls' voices get too loud, he rushes in, yells at them above *their* yelling, and either appoints himself judge and jury or sends them both to their rooms for the rest of the evening because, "If I've told you once, I've told you a thousand times, stop this screaming and bickering!" Neither of these interventions have any significant positive or lasting effect on their arguments, although there is temporary quiet in the Normal household. (And, some days, temporary quiet is a *very* desirable condition.) The silence is usually short because the girls soon start whining and begging to regain their freedom and Hal gives in just to stop the whining (which is almost as bad as the original bickering.) Then the home is calm, respectful, and loving — for at least fifteen minutes.

On one particular night, after Hal had lectured the girls and sent them to their rooms forever, Hal awoke about 2:00 a.m. to find a strange, one-foot-tall, orange creature on his headboard (who somehow reminded him of his wife when she offered her words of wisdom). The creature told him about the ineffective way he handled Cindy's and Mindy's arguments. The creature talked of boundaries and emotional buttons in practical terms.

"First," it began, "try to stay out of their battles more often. Their arguments will not hurt you. Turn off your button that says anger is dangerous. *As long as the kids fight fairly, do not get involved in the solutions.* Their disagreements are not your issue. However, I do advise you to listen from nearby occasionally to be sure that they eventually reach a mutual and fair resolution.

"Second," the little orange thing continued, "do not be judge and jury. When you do that, either Cindy or Mindy will feel she was cheated by you or that you ignored her feelings. At best, the other knows she manipulated you to take her side.

"Third, when their noise level really gets to you, tell them, as calmly as possible, to keep their voices down — their racket *is your issue.* Then if they do not comply by quieting down, a short time-out to their rooms is appropriate as well as good for your sanity.

"Last, you can offer them an incentive for cooperating

with your need for peace. For example, tell the girls that when they have argued *quietly* ten times - and not ten in a row - with some occasional *reminders* from you or Sal, that you will take them out for their very own mushroom pizza. Of course, they will stage some false disagreements just to earn their reward, but consider that they actually are practicing doing what you want you want them to do. Eventually, this will cut out half of their screaming fights. Expecting any more improvement than that is beyond even Walt Disney's happiest endings."

The creature smiled and vanished. Hal did not tell Sal or the girls about what happened that night. Over the next few weeks, the Normal females noticed how Hal, and the girls' arguments, had slowly become less volatile and noisy. And the girls thanked Hal for being the best father in the world, between bites of pizza, of course.

*****

I am sure it required large doses of courage, self-discipline, and humility for Hal to try the creature's suggestions. The little orange guy would be on my positive parenting consultant list even though I have no idea how to call him. As an aside, had I awakened and seen this weird being near my head, I probably would have jumped a mile or smothered him with my pillow. Creatures should be more careful about sneaking around strangers in the middle of the night.

When we give our children a command, often our first reaction to any disagreement, groan, or complaint they make is to respond from a position of authority by saying, "Because I'm the mother (or father), that's why!" In school or in public places, there are authority figures to whom our children should respond with a quick, "Yes, Sir/Ma'am." At home, however, we need to let them express their dissatisfactions as long as there is an air of respect in their tone. Try to breathe a bit as they spout their feelings and opinions. If necessary, after the issue is resolved (which does not necessarily mean they agree with your final decision), explain how disagreements should be phrased with appropriate respectfulness. But remember to discuss the style of conversation after the discussion of the initial topic is completed. To focus on a child's intonation during the initial conversation is to ignore the value of his point by abusing your arbitrary power of parenthood. Your victory, therefore, is hollow — and resentment is building somewhere.

The Normals Revisited

This story focuses on Sal and *her problem* with the kids' battles. For Sal, it was little Joey's misery when he claimed his older sisters picked on him two-against-one. One night, while the three children were playing their video games, Joey screeched about the girls not letting him have his turn. Sal stomped in, as usual, and told the girls to stop teaming up against their younger (i.e., poor, little, helpless, etc.) brother. Usually, the girls acquiesced, Joey dried his crocodile tears, and that was that.

Tonight, as preadolescents are wont to do more often as

part of their normal development, Cindy blew up at Sal (who was not comfortable about being at the receiving end of her daughter's anger — but then, who is?). "Mom, you always think that Joey is so innocent. Get real! He gets his fair share of turns, but acts like he is being swindled and tortured just so you will rush in and get him what he wants. Believe it or not, sometimes Mindy and Joey pick on me. In fact, sometimes Joey and me... never mind — I'd never be unfair to *my* beloved brother and sister."

Sal practiced her breathing and did her best not to interrupt Cindy. She mostly listened. Finally, Sal responded as calmly as possible, "You may have a point, Cindy. I'll sleep on it. For now, you can all just roll some dice to decide whose turn it is and who goes after that." Sal added a final hint not to argue with their mother any more tonight and to do as they were told. *Middle childhooders will frequently surprise us with their level-headedness.* In this instance, the children found some dice and did as they were told.

Later that night, as Sal stepped out of the shower and wrapped herself in a large towel, the little orange creature was waiting for her next to the sink. Sal patted the thing's head as though she were petting the family cat, "You're kinda cute, little fella. What can I do for you?" The creature seemed to enjoy the stroking — just the way we human creatures do. "You know, Sal, your daughter was mostly right tonight about how Joey manipulates you."

"Oh. It's just as simple as that is it?" Sal responded with a hint of frustration in her voice. "And how many little creatures have you raised to gain such expertise?"

"Enough to be credible," it replied. "First, Joey gets a lot of mileage from being the baby of the family and he uses this position to his advantage whenever he can. Cindy uses her "I'm the oldest and most responsible" act when she wants extra privileges. Mindy uses her "I'm the middle child, nothing special about me, poor me" bit when trying to wriggle out of trouble. These are greatly realistic roles due to their perceptions of their relationships to each other, and the way we tend set expectations and hopes for our children by their order of birth. But don't let them play you for a fool because of their order. Each rung on the birth ladder has its pros and cons.

Sal got a bit defensive and referred to her own childhood. "Not *all* kids do that! I did not do that kind of stuff to my parents when I was a kid."

"Oh, no?" the creature queried. "Remember when your older brother got to go to the baseball game with your dad and you didn't because you were *too young* and because you were *a girl?*" Remember how you used your "girl's can enjoy sports as much as guys" and "he gets everything because he's the oldest" routines to get that slumber party out of your mom as well as the trip to the movies out of your dad?"

Sal snorted, "How do you know about that! Anyway, you forgot the super fudge sundae I made my brother buy me after I made him feel guilty, too."

The orange thing continued, "Second, kids also compete for your attention and support just because you and Hal are the parents. Kids naturally fear that there may be limited love and affection available from their parents and they want to be sure they get at least their fair share. It's called sibling rivalry. Your job is to try to be fair in what you give them while not letting them force you into keeping a scorecard of who got what, when, and how much time and money was spent on whom.

"Last, it is also normal for siblings to try to manipulate their parents by playing one against another. Encourage them to solve their own problems which includes *you staying out of their problems when possible.* If you can do this, which is no small task, Joey and the girls will find fair solutions on their own more often. When they have difficulty finding a solution, or a quick solution is best, a hint like using dice (i.e., settle it by using luck) is helpful. Don't stay out of their problems — just don't go flying in when you aren't really needed.

*****

Do not rush to solve disagreements for your children that they may be able to solve for themselves. This theory applies to both sibling arguments and individual tasks. Be available to help them find better solutions but, avoid finding the actual answer for them unless you are convinced they cannot solve the problem independently or with appropriate speed for their ages. Even then, only give as much help as needed to get them started or when they get stuck. Offer to help when you feel they need it. Of course, be sure to give tons of support and encouragement.

The previous article's summary includes the idea of being available for the teachable moments when you can educate or share your life experiences with your children. Use these moments to build rapport and give touches — physical and emotional — of love, affection, sympathy, and pride. Middle childhooders are still very willing to give and accept in-home displays of affection, though certainly not in front of their peers. The way you initiate and receive hugs and kisses is a major means of teaching how you believe they should respect themselves and others regarding physical touch and affection. The other way you teach your children about touch and also about romance is how you and your spouse (or serious relationship if you are a single parent) interact physically with each other.

The Normals After Dark

The kids were asleep and the late news was over. Hal turned toward Sal and untied the bow on her nightgown. "I thought you were tired," she giggled.

As they began breathing heavily, Hal was distracted by something moving next to his pillow. You-Know-Who had returned. Sal sighed with the same disappointment Hal felt. "What is it now?" she said.

"You know," their visitor began, "this is a good time to discuss teaching reproduction and sexuality to the kids. It is not something you tell them in one big lecture like it was done back in the old days. You tell the children in small doses, and tell them often when opportunities arise in ads, movies, TV shows, the news, what you see in the park, and so on. There are books for parents and also for children of both sexes and for various ages to help you out, too. The more naturally you treat the subject, the more normally your children will accept sex and love as the natural part of life that it is. You also have to cover how to treat others with respect physically and romantically, keeping your dignity at the same time. *And* that a girl does not owe any boy a night of sex just because he took her to a movie. *And* that boys can say "no" too. *And* that both of you need to explain reproduction to all the kids, not just Hal talking to Joey and Sal to the girls. *And...*"

"*And* get lost, you little creep!" Hal and Sal said in unison. The creature disappeared. The pesky orange thing reminded them of the times when the kids came in the bedroom while they were in mid-ecstasy.

Sometimes they could regain the passion immediately after an interruption. Sometimes not. Sal gave Hal a peck an the lips and he pecked back. That would be it for tonight. Sometimes our kids are little orange creatures.

*****

When teaching your children about reproduction, sensuality, and accompanying sexual activity, try to keep the ethical and biological aspects separate issues. Present the physical and scientific information repeatedly throughout childhood, especially during the pre-pubescent and the puberty onset years of middle childhood. Do the same with your moral values regarding sexual behavior. Use books or tapes often, letting them have their own books to look at in private. Do not just read the texts to your children, but add comments and answer questions as needed. *Admit when you learn something* you had not known before to model the idea that none of us knows everything about the world of sex. *Agree to find answers* for any questions for which you do not have a clear or updated answer. Admit when you are embarrassed but keep the discussion going. They know you are rattled anyway. Your honesty and sincerity are worth untold bonus points in the long run for everyone.

So, let's say you are the father and are not entirely comfortable explaining reproductive anatomy to your eleven-year-old soon-to-start-menstruating daughter. (Not surprisingly, such conversations with her were probably easier for you when she was only seven years old.) At such times, hold this discussion with both parents present and or get some books to help get the chat going. Of course, same sex parent-child discussions are needed, too. Special father-son and mother-daughter talks are necessary for modeling and sex identity bonding. We dads cannot fully understand women's biology since we don't have a female body. The same is true for moms with their sons. Talk to your spouse (and other About Me Book consultants listed under sex education) about your discomforts.

The Unwanted Cavalry: Back At The (Normal's) Ranch

"I did not need your help. I was doing just fine!" Sal was hot, talking fast.

Hal was not too calm himself. "Mindy was getting the best of you. You were being too soft on her."

"Mindy does best with her homework when I handle her softly. You're good with Joey and his schoolwork, but Mindy requires a different touch. Your way is *not the only way*, you know!" Her voice was loud. "Anyway," she continued, "you shouldn't have butted in with Mindy right there. I felt humiliated and undermined as though you were the expert, which, by the way, you ain't!" She was furious and hurt, too.

Hal was about to respond when the creature appeared. — "It's him, again."

"How do you know it's a 'him'?" Sal demanded. "You think you know everything today!"

"Actually, I'm neither he nor she," it said slowly, trying to calm their testy moods. "I'm a *skeeg*, but that is not important now. What *is important* is for both of you to acknowledge that you are good parents and have continued to improve since my first visit almost a year ago. But sometimes you both get overly confident that you know more than the other one does."

"Ain't that the truth!" spat Sal, her emotional temperature still high.

The creature ignored her comment. "Both of you are proud and protective of your ability to effectively handle your children. *Both of you* have strengths and weaknesses with each of your children. And *both of you* can benefit by insights from the other."

It paused to breathe, or whatever it is that skeegs do. "The problem, and both of you have it at times, is that you come flying to the rescue when the other parent did not announce any emergency."

Hal lowered his eyes and mumbled, "Kind of like an unwanted cavalry."

Sal put her hand on Hal's shoulder. "The thing said that both of us play cavalry. How about from here on, if I don't call for you, just bite your lip, run around the block, whatever, but keep out of it. You can *give me hints afterward and I'll give your hints consideration.* And I will do I likewise with you."

The orange thing cocked its head sideways like those dogs do in movies. "I call this process of giving each other helpful hints 'coaching.' I use this term since an effective coach helps others maximize their strengths while minimizing their weaknesses through the insights of a perceptive observer. The coach does not directly interfere on the field unless the parent-in-action requests or there really is an actual emergency such as abuse taking place.

The coach is allowed to come into the fray and ask the parent-in-action if he or she wants an immediate consult. If the answer is 'yes' then both parents disengage from the child, but *only to discuss the immediate situation.* In addition, and this is very important for parenting teamwork, if the parent-in-action does not want the consult, the coach backs off. Both parents need to be aware of past buttons brewing in the present. Beware of emotions running too high." The orange guy caught his breath. "As to this cavalry solution, you Normals solved it yourselves. I'm almost out of a job here." Then he vanished.

Over the next few years, Sal and Hal played unwanted cavalry much less than they did before that visit by the skeeg creature. Usually they thanked each other *for butting out,* since they both knew it was *not easy* to do: not easy at all.

*****

Coaching *without* insisting you are right (which implies your parenting partner is wrong) is no easy process when feelings are raw for whatever reason. The coach and spouse may need multiple breathing breaks. Some families devise a hand signal between parents that means, "freeze and breathe." For a coach to do more *when not invited or wanted* is to be more of a domineering power player than a helper. Remember that sometimes you are the coach and other times you are the parent-in-action in need of some coaching.

At some point, our middle childhood children grow up, graduate from high school, go to college, move out, get jobs, get married, and so forth. In other words, they become mature citizens who will make adult decisions, balance checkbooks, and make successful lives for themselves. It is important to keep this in mind because some days this concept will seem incomprehensible. Much of parenting contains mixed emotions. Observing our children's development and maturity also shadows our own development, aging, and need to reset our personal goals as the kids move onward to independence. As usual, no easy task.

Pomp & Circumstance

"I should be happy. Our oldest daughter is graduating tonight." Sal buttoned her dress slowly as if trying to keep time from moving forward.

Hal spoke sympathetically as he straightened his tie. "What is the matter?"

"Cindy did well as a student. She was on the drill team and played basketball. She has a lot of friends. Her boyfriend, Freddie, is as nice as can be." Sal paused. "I should be happy for her and proud of her. Instead I am feeling sad, empty."

She spied the little orange creature peeking from behind her tissue box. "I hope you have some words of wisdom, little guy. Feeling bad on a joyous occasion does not make sense to me."

"It does to me," he began in a most tender voice. "Cindy is going off to college in the fall. This graduation signals her leaving you. Your job for eighteen years, raising one of your children, is over in many ways. You taught her how to fly and now she is going to do it. You are losing both a part of

her and a piece of yourself. Why shouldn't you feel sad?"

Hal put his hand on Sal's shoulder. "Sal, you once said that although you had always wanted to get married, you simultaneously regretted our wedding because your freedom was gone in some ways."

Sal brushed her cheek across his hand. " I don't regret it at all now."

Hal smiled and continued, "You admitted the same thing when Cindy was born. And you felt guilty for feeling that way then, too. You were overjoyed to have a baby, but saddened at the *loss of the privacy* you and I had gotten used to."

The room was silent for a moment.

The creature spoke next. "All through your development — *a process that never ends* — you have to give up pieces of your prior self to make room for new parts. Cindy cannot have the security of home and the freedom of college life at the same time. Soon, you will find new pieces of you that had been forgotten, put in your mental closet, or you never knew were inside you. And part of those pieces will be a new relationship with Cindy. Don't resist family and personal developmental change at any stage. *Go with it.* You cannot stop it. Try not to face change alone."

Sal smiled at the creature. "Who are you anyway?"

"I am your own voice of wisdom. Sometimes you both give superb advice to others when they ask for help. But under pressure, you do not always follow the path of parenting and teamwork that you already know. I put together those ideas, thoughts, and sayings, along with a few of my own, and give them to you when you need them.

"You mean I need to listen to myself more often?"

"Yes," it continued, "but that is not easy to do. If you could do it all the time you would be a perfect parent and *you know that perfection is impossible.* Even if you could be the absolutely flawless mother, all that perfection would go to waste unless you had perfect children and a perfect husband to live with you. You are just fine the way you are."

The creature bowed to them and disappeared. The family went to Cindy's graduation. Mindy looked around at boys. Joey fidgeted at times, and although Hal and Sal felt both pride and sadness, they *mostly* felt pride.

*****

The Normals are a normal and healthy family. Their ups usually stay up and their downs do not stay down very long. Hal and Sal are ever improving at being each other's little orange coaches. With their increased skills at breathing to ten and differentiating between real emergencies and emotional buttons, both Hal and Sal are proud of themselves, their marriage, and their family. As the curtain closes on the Normals, Hal and Sal are writing their own names in their About Me Books along with each other's on their consultant lists — on the positive page the vast majority of the time, of course.

SECTION 3:

INTRODUCTION TO MENTAL HEALTH PROBLEMS

Even In the healthiest families, emotional and behavioral problems can exist on either a temporary or chronic basis. In the last section of this book, I will describe my favorite interventions with middle childhood trouble spots. In this section, the focus is on mental health situations in which professional help from medical, pastoral, educational, or mental health experts may be necessary during the middle childhood years.

As with any difficulty, as already discussed in the chapter on About Me Books, it is a strength to know when to seek needed consultants. Further, when in doubt, call the experts early. Usually, there will be fairly quick results that will free you and your children to do projects you would rather be doing — and to be doing those things more happily and efficiently. In addition, most problems take longer to correct the longer they continue. Equally, the sooner they are addressed, the easier the remediation and healing will be.

Parents and teachers are somehow, almost magically, supposed to have insight and practical expertise in everything involving children. Talk about perfectionistic stress! This chapter is not meant to make you a mental health diagnostician but rather to help you discern everyday concerns from more serious conditions — to tell the normal bumps and bruises of middle childhood from true emergencies.

Getting Help For Your Children

Depression, anxiety, severely codependent relationships, and the various behavior problems described in this section usually require professional intervention. Below is a list of behaviors and emotions that are signals for further evaluation:

1. *ongoing* disobedience or disrespect to any parent or authority;

2. lowered academic effort or concentration;

3. continued sadness and lack of energy;

4. habitual excuses or blaming;

5. regularly denying appropriate responsibility;

6. low esteem, especially when in *multiple areas;*

7. immaturity in handling successes (winning) and failures (losing);

8. short attention span, easy distractibility;

9. ongoing (and unfounded) physical complaints;

10. manipulation of others *with lack of assertion;*

11. persistent fears and phobias (specific fears);

12. ritual behavior alone or in peer groups;

13. unresolved guilt;

14. unresolved grief or denied feelings of grief;

15. moodiness, excessive anger/temper;

16. inability to relax, have fun, or have appropriate humor;

17. problems compromising and sharing with peers;

18. frequent impulsivity;

19. perceived helplessness, presumed victimization.

When in doubt about the severity of your child's problem, consult a mental health professional who specializes with children or families through your school counselor, pediatrician, church minister, police juvenile officer, or your insurance office. Here are some basic guidelines for getting effective professional help. Seek someone who has professional training and experience *and specializes* in child and/or adolescent problems. The specific professional degree (social work, psychiatry, psychology, counseling) is not as important when compared to experience. However, there are a number of types of professionals in the mental health field, having somewhat different specialties, with some providing certain services that the others do not offer.

Psychiatrists are physicians specializing in the medical aspects of mental illness and human biology. Many also have training in counseling although few provide counseling sessions nowadays. At this time, only physicians (M.D. or D.O.) can prescribe medications. Be cautious if a psychiatrist or pediatrician *arbitrarily* either insists on the use of medications or demands that medications never be used for any particular condition. There are always various factors to be considered in deciding whether medicines are to be used as part of the treatment — and medication is *only a part* of effective mental health treatment. Undoubtedly, when medications are necessary, it is not fair to you or to your child for you, the parent, to automatically withhold or insist upon them.

Social Workers specialize in looking at the total child — his family, his friendships, and community resources, including schools (consulting with the school when needed). Their counseling usually includes the child, siblings, and the parents, and looks at the ways in which the parental relationship has an impact on the child, depending upon the issues at hand. The social work emphasis is on the child and the various factors and people impacting upon that child. Social workers can have an M.S.W. degree (masters of arts in social work), Ph.D. (doctorate of philosophy in social work), or D.S.W. (doctorate in social work) degree. Most states also have license requirements to practice.

Psychologists specialize in diagnostics, testing and assessment, in addition to usually having expertise in counseling of individuals, couples, and/or families. Some psychologists have special expertise in schools. Psychologists may have Ph.D., Psy.D (doctorate in clinical treatment), Ed.D.(doctorate of education specializing in psychology), or M.A. (masters) degrees.

In most states there are additional licenses for mental health professionals trained to help children including licensed professional counselors, pastoral counselors, school counselors, and psychiatric nurses. Almost always, these licenses cover experts with at least a master's level degree. Wherever you live, ask the practitioner what his or her specialty is and how long her or she has been in practice. Often it is wise to talk to two professionals before making your choice.

Most professionals, regardless of their degree or license,

work with other experts. For example, my license is in clinical social work (master's degree level) with a specialization in children and families. I have personally added an M.A.T. (master of arts in teaching) to further specialize in behavioral, social, and emotional problems which occur in school. When necessary, I refer the family to a psychiatrist to assess the need for medication, to a psychologist to assess for learning disabilities or personality problems, or to a neurologist or occupational therapist to assess impulse and coordination deficits. At times, I refer to various psychological, educational, or medical experts to get a second opinion as to what may be causing or influencing the child's problem. Then I continue the counseling depending upon what the expert's evaluation reveals. Further, there are issues that I do not consider appropriate for me to treat, such as the counseling of a sexually abused teenage girl. I will refer her to a more expert, and female, colleague, although I am licensed to see that girl. Where sexual privacy, issues of feminine identity and molestation by a male adult is involved, I believe specialized treatment is required and that a female therapist is better and more appropriate in being a nurturing and less threatening agent for the recovery of the client's renewed sense of assertion and security in life than a male therapist can be for sexually victimized girls. It is in situations like these in which a professional's expertise and years of experience far outweigh the therapist's specific degree.

Remember that *you are a consumer* and the therapist is the service provider. Ask any questions you have — *any* questions.

View your therapist as a mental health consultant from whom you get information and feedback, and with whom you will explore and treat the problems that exist in your family. Mutual respect with your counselor is paramount to success. If your therapist insists on controlling the issues, tell him or her of your feelings.

*****

If you feel there is a problem at your home, there probably is one. *When in doubt, get it checked out.*

Depression, anxiety (as in chronic worry), and Attention Deficit Disorder (ADD which sometimes includes hyperactivity and is then abbreviated as ADHD) are like three circles overlapping at the center. They all have a number of factors in common. Yet, because of the differences in their outer parts of each circle, they are all handled differently when our children are burdened by any one of them. The last section of Middle Childhood looks at various interventions to help with these problems and when to use them to help your child cope with these and other emotional and behavioral problems of childhood.

Depression And Anxiety

Depression is an emotional and cognitive distortion based upon the child's assumption, real or imagined, that he has failed in the past and that his failures will continue in the future. Depression is, at the least, an attitude of inability by the child to improve his own unhappy condition. Cognition is the process by which we learn, become aware of, and interpret our world, and the manner in which we remind ourselves of our abilities, failings, and talents. For example, a boy we will name Steven may be an average soccer player on his sixth grade team. His cognitive comments to himself may be, "I'm a pretty good player, especially at defense. Sometimes, I wish I were better." His cognitions about this aspect of his life sound quite accurate. However, his cognitions become distorted when he either inflates his view by saying, "I'm the greatest. This team would lose every game if I didn't show up," or by devaluing his importance by telling himself, "They don't really need me. I'm no good. They'd win more games if stayed I home sick." When more severe, depression becomes a conviction of situational hopelessness in which no one else can help to ameliorate his pain either. The child distorts his unrealistic and negative view about himself (cognitions) so even non failures are believed to be failures. His mood becomes further depressed and his view further distorted in a downward spiral.When that same eleven-year-old boy is dropped from his soccer team for repeatedly arguing with his coach and referees, *his depressed mood is realistic according to his experience* (whether or not the consequence he received was deserved). A few days of moping is normal regardless of the cause of his loss. If his ongoing reaction is that he is unlovable, that he is undeserving of acceptance by others, then serious depression may exist. A child's attitude of helplessness and hopelessness may also be in response to problems in schoolwork, sports, loss of a friend, or death of a relative. Depression cannot be argued away regardless of the persuasiveness of the parent's statements.

The prevention for depression involves installing positive perspective. With perspective he can see that there is balance in life and, for the most part, things go well for him. The most effective parental responses to a continued depressed mood are *tender loving care through listening* and by helping replace his consistently negative statements to himself with more positive comments. Do not force the completion of tasks or focus on performance. The depression causes the child to have little physical energy. Further, he is emotionally *convinced* that success is beyond his control as part of his condition. Since he feels helpless to succeed, disciplinary consequences are usually of little use in dealing with depression. Try to keep extended discussions away from the negatives of the past since positive perspective is gained through living in the present and *planning realistically* for the future. A review of the past is helpful to lower reoccurrences of failures.If the child refuses such discussions, it is certainly time to seek professional mental health assistance.

Anxiety is a different loss of perspective wherein the

child remains overly and nervously focused in the future. Commonly, it is called worry. With a pinch of uncomfortable anxiety as a motivator, the non over-anxious child will make a plan to avoid mishaps and failures. A bite of emotional discomfort as a natural consequence motivates a child to do things differently the next time. However, when the child's continuing fear of failure interferes with his completion of regular tasks and his participation with peers, then his anxiety is beyond his self-control to turn off the worries in his mind. As with depression, a parent cannot convince an over-anxious child to stop his obsessions.

The ongoing prevention for ongoing anxiety is the avoiding of endless worrisome talk and giving only limited attention to trivial complaints and excuses. With anxiety there exists an abundance of potential emergencies. This does not mean you should ignore the fears of your child. However, his fearful chatter should be limited by focusing, with help from you, on what he can do in the present to lower his worries about tomorrow. Be wary of excuses for incomplete work. Do not stress perfect work: his anxious pattern is proof that he is already a perfectionist, afraid to make the slightest mistake. Encourage stress reduction activities, such as counting to ten or playing a non competitive game activity such as working on puzzles. For example, one of your eight-year-old twin daughters does not do well on weekly spelling tests but is not concerned. "When I grow up, pencils and pens will have built-in spell-check so it won't let me misspell words. I don't need to know how to spell well." She *should be worried* more and studying harder. Simultaneously, if her twin sister does well on all tests, including spelling, but worries about failing third grade altogether, this is an over-anxious response. The studious twin has a mental domino effect in mind: "If I fail a spelling test, then I might fail math. Then I'll fail high school and never go to college, and then I won't ever get a good job." She needs a loving yet guiding parental approach to help

THIS BOY MAY BE DEPRESSED, CONVINCED HE CANNOT DO HIS WORK. HE MAY BE ANXIOUS, WORRYING ABOUT HOW HIS PARENTS WILL REACT TO HIS LOW TEST GRADE WHEREBY HIS ABILITY TO FOCUS FOR THE ENTIRE LENGTH OF THE TASK IS IMPAIRED. OR, HE MAY BE ANGRY AND DEFIANT. LAST, HE MAY HAVE A COLD AND JUST FEEL TIRED.

slow this panic. If she is unable to ease her worry and has a pattern of jumping from one worry to another this is a signal to seek a professional consultation. (Come to think of it, if the first twin continues to refuse to study spelling after firm talks by you and her teacher, I would seek out the school counselor for her also.) At times, childhood depression and anxiety continue too long or with too much intensity. Depression and anxiety problems can exist at any age — I have seen many severely unhappy or nervous children under the age of three. When depression or anxiety are too intense, the child loses his ability to function smoothly in the present by being too emotionally locked in past misery or worry of the future. When the problems become too extreme he responds by worrying or complaining more than working on the tasks: thus he cannot earn sufficient self-credits to strive for further effort and success — two major building blocks of self-esteem.

*****

If you are concerned that your child may have ongoing or intense depression and/or anxiety, have the problem assessed by a qualified and experienced professional. Both anxiety and depression are highly treatable through counseling, mental health education, and, when needed, medication therapy. This theme of not ignoring problems and *getting help early when a problem does not respond to what usually works* may sound like repetitive advice. It is. Getting help is important to keeping a healthier family healthy and to helping a codependent family make healthy gains.

Unlike depression and anxiety, most of the indicators of ADHD (Attention Deficit Hyperactivity Disorder) are more behavioral than emotional. To stand on my soapbox for a moment, I prefer to call this condition "ADC" for Attention Deficit Condition. <u>ADHD has strengths</u> of intelligence, quick thinking, humor, creativity, intense attention to certain tasks, and vivid imagination that do not fall under the term "disorder." Interestingly, these same strengths are the problems of the child with ADHD by occurring when not wanted — much like blades of grass making up a beautiful lawn are considered weeds in your garden and how the dandelion marring that same lawn is a blowable toy to a young child.

ADHD - Attention Deficit Hyperactivity Disorder

ADHD is a psychological, psychiatric, and neurological condition characterized by poor organization, difficulty in paying attention (especially when the child is bored), difficulty being distracted when immersed in a task he is interested in, impulsivity, overactivity sometimes to the point that the child is physically unable to sit still as long as his peers can, and difficulty switching smoothly from one activity to another. ADHD is observable on brain scans and easily confirmed by computerized tests created specifically to assess it. ADHD is usually diagnosable through a combination of school records, teacher and parent rating scales, and observations and interviews by specialists dealing with ADHD at school, home, or in a clinical office. ADHD, for better and worse, is a lifelong condition.

Numerous medications when needed, used together with behavioral counseling, can be very effective in helping the deficits of ADHD become assets. On my soapbox again, medication is frequently given too quickly when behavioral intervention alone may be adequate. When actual hyperactivity — the physical inability to stay still — exists, medication use is almost always needed. To not use medication when it is required, holds the child unfairly responsible for behavior for which he is not fully responsible. Note: ADHD makes many types of task more difficult, but not impossible. *I do not want people of any age having ADHD to use their condition as an excuse to avoid doing what is expected, but they should receive the extra services to help them.* (Having ADHD myself, I say this with the strongest conviction.) The vast majority of people with ADHD do *not* also have hyperactivity.

People with ADHD have an actual breakdown in the parts of the brain responsible for the organization of materials, time, and ideas. The ADHD may be so mild that it is only seen at school in personally frustrating tasks and subjects. There is the more severe ADHD affecting all areas of schoolwork and homework, social relationships, and functioning at home.

The breakdown of organization makes keeping priorities in place more difficult. Thus the child with ADHD is more distractible than other children. There is what I call the "yo-yo imagination." Let's say your child's class is discussing Florida and the teacher mentions Disneyworld. Every student's mind flies off to the Magic Kingdom in dreamy distraction. (Daydreams are normal and healthy for all of us.) Like a yo-yo, most of the students' thoughts come back shortly to the teacher's continuing lecture. They can keep the priority of the class topic foremost in their minds especially if the information is to be on an upcoming test. The child with ADHD may not spring back to the lecture as his strong imagination may take over and create marvelous trip itineraries lasting many minutes. As he daydreams, he loses his previously and sincerely set priority to listen for what will be on tomorrow's test. Because his internal sense of time organization is also weak, he does not realize how long he has been daydreaming. In contrast, when the class topic is of interest to him, when he is physically healthy, and when there are no strange noises outside the classroom, the ADHD child may keep his attention on the topic as well as anyone else in the class. The more mild his ADHD is, the more inconsistently it effects his behavior. Mild afflictions of any type are usually more difficult to identify — and thus correct — since the problematic symptoms are not evident on a regular basis.

Further, there is a problem at the other end of the attention spectrum that I call "tunnel focus," whereby his intense interest becomes focused to the point that he cannot be distracted as easily as the other students. He can have difficulty changing from subject to subject when he is immersed in the present task. The child with ADHD may have trouble going down the hall from his classroom to the gymnasium or to the cafeteria. These changes may be worst when he had been engrossed in a task just prior to having to move to another place. Giving him advanced warnings — not threats — before the changes is often helpful, much like the snooze button on the alarm clock gives us repeated notice that we really do have to get out of bed soon. Such reminders let the ADHD child slowly pull away from the immediate task and prepare himself to deal with a change in place or activity.

Impulsivity is acting before thinking and is an aspect of ADHD that interferes with self-control. He runs into the street after the ball before he can remind himself to look for traffic first. The ADHD child thinks the same ideas as the other children in wanting to get the ball, only his peers either stop to check for traffic or are watching for it as they approach the street. The child with ADHD suffers from the "broken garage door" syndrome wherein while the other children, for example, withhold insults they are tempted to use in anger, the child with ADHD blurts them out before the garage door can close and keep the ill-timed comments in. As with the ball rolling toward the oncoming cars, the ADHD child focuses on the ball and ignores the cues of the upcoming sidewalk and screams from friends. His friends can stop themselves when necessary to wait and let the ball roll onward.

With all these complications of self-control and attention-span, it is common to see sibling and peer problems develop due to not waiting patiently for a turn at the drinking fountain, daydreaming at home plate in kickball, misunderstanding game rules, and overreacting to teasing with anger or hurt feelings. A major result of organizational breakdown is difficulty in solving the problems in school, home, and on the playground. Mix in the short attention span when bored and frustrated and it is understandable that the ADHD child is more likely to repeat errors and less likely to repeat successes. Depression is common in the child with ADHD because he does not understand why he is picked on and why he continues to get into trouble of various sorts. He feels like a victim because, and, due to a problem over which he has little control, *he is a victim.*

In addition, he repeatedly hears the "P-word": *potential.* He is smart and often capable of superior work when the conditions are right for his style of learning. Use of the P-word, in actuality, is a backhanded way of saying, "He's a failure." We need to convince the child with ADHD that although he does have failings, *he is not a failure.* We need to help him realize and remember his strengths.

*****

Now the good news! Place the child with ADHD in a setting where he is at his best, give him needed structure to complete tasks, teach him how to handle his ADHD for his age, correct his deficits with time, and he will shine and be proud. His imagination just may win him awards.

Note: If the above chapter sounded like *your biography*, as well as that of your child, that is because ADHD runs in families at least half the time. Get help for yourself along with your son or daughter and become a coaching team as Hal and Sal Normal did. Remember, ADHD's deficits stay with you for life. But *so do the strengths*!

The following chapter is about normal grieving in healthier families. Hal and Sal Normal handled their daughter's high school graduation as both a time of loss and of celebration. Most moments of grief contain a mixture of emotions. Grief has its own emotional issues which become more complicated or eased by our personalities or learning styles. When a beloved grandparent dies, we are saddened at their death yet, at the same time, hold warm memories of good times with them. The more sudden and unexpected the death or loss, the greater our negative feelings of surprise, disbelief, fright, and even horror and anger in situations in which violence and crime are involved. With depressed children, the losses are grieved with even greater intensity and length. The overly anxious child frets over impending future losses beyond what is expected for his age or situationally-appropriate levels of concern. Sometimes, the anxious child reacts instead by not grieving but rather by focusing on the feelings of others. The ADHD child's reactions range from a tunnel focus similar to depression to apparent disregard through distraction.

Saying Goodbye

There are four basic stages of grief to complete before a child can continue with his life after a loss. Stage one is *Denial and Shock* whereby he does not fully accept that the person or life dream (something he had always hoped for) is dead, although he may shed many tears at the time. For example, an eight-year old boy's dog has been run over by a car. He is horrified by the gory image he envisions. He may experience intense guilt if he feels he should not have let the dog out of the yard or that somehow he should have been present to protect his pet. The dog's violent death may represent the deaths of parents or other incidents he cannot prevent but that will someday occur. The feelings, are initially too intense for the child to accept the event as really having happened. Stage two is *Anger-Sadness* about the loss. The child can be angry because the death occurred at an inopportune time for him, perhaps before he got to say something he wanted to say, or because he feels deserted and helpless. As another example, Grandpa may have died suddenly and the nine-year-old granddaughter may have planned to go fishing with him the following week. At this stage she can begin to feel her emotions but they are still mostly uncomfortable. Stage three is characterized by *Deep Sorrow* and its accompanying situational depression. During this phase rest, reminiscing, and quiet discomfort are most prominent and are necessary in cleansing out the hurt slowly. Although the parents may have been separated for a few months already when the divorce is finalized, the twelve-year-old girl or boy may spend much time alone, crying, watching TV, or talking to friends about the parental breakup. Much of this grief is over the death of his family arrangement even though both parents my be attentive and keep their visits on schedule. Stage four is a *Rebuilding* phase during which the child accepts the loss and reorients to life today, focusing on future goals once more. The closer the relationship or the larger the dream, the more intense the emotions of these stages will be. Temporary guilt is common in adjusting to any death. We feel we did not spend enough time or resolve a disagreement. The eleven-year-old whose mother died of cancer now realizes that her mother had loved ceramics, so she will take up ceramics in school. She spends increased time with a maternal aunt to help build her identity as a woman in the family.

There are many forms of loss: physical death of a parent, grandparent, friend, or pet; relationship death when someone a child idolizes is forced from a pedestal; death of a dream when a parent's job is lost, a parent is injured, or the hope for the future goal becomes impossible to achieve.

Divorce is now the most common form of childhood grief because it entails death of the physical family structure, the death of regular contact with both parents, and the death of the hope of keeping a perfect family as the child knows it. Often, the more dysfunctional the family relationships, the harder it is for the child to reach stage four of the grieving process. Such a child can become stuck in depression. He may emotionally reside in an intermittent stage two and a half, called *Bargaining,* in which the child pleads with his parents, God, whomever, to trade something for fixing the family. He may promise to always do his homework without complaining or promise to never tease his dog again. Bargaining is a fantasy of assumed power, since no child is responsible for, nor can prevent, a divorce although he often easily accepts responsibility and guilt. Due to development, the child sees himself as central to all issues that involve him. Emotionally, for the child, there is no such thing as a "good" divorce, although there are certainly times when divorce is necessary for the mental health of one of the spouses.

Unfortunately, during divorce, the time that the child needs his parents attention and patient structure the most is when the parents can easily *and understandably* be focused on their own emotional needs. When there is dysfunction, parents may focus primarily upon their own loss while less able to focus upon their children's needs for nurturing parents to continue the previous stability of routines and to lead the family into the future with goals, standards, and expectations. Children require honesty from us. Do not deny feelings and tears they observe in order to "protect them." To tell children you are not upset when you clearly are upset merely *confuses them* or models for them that they *should not* talk about uncomfortable feelings. Share your fears and concerns openly *on their level* without making the children your counselors. If there is a death of an adult they know, you may be tempted to promise not to die. Do not promise what you cannot actually guarantee. But do share reassurances that are true.

Each child grieves individually to loss, at times in unexpected and unpredictable ways. Grieving, like any emotion, will reappear later if squelched or discouraged when initially appearing. The best help for a grieving child is patient listening offered for as long as the child deems necessary. A burial ceremony of mementos, poems, and whatever, can be helpful in moving the grieving process toward the stage of acceptance. An upcoming section on development will help you spot emotional regression — a phase in which your children may act as they did when they were younger. Such behavior is common when children deal with grief. If you insist that your child "grow up and act your age" — even if said in a loving tone — you unwittingly lengthen her grief although her surface behavior may change according to your request.

*****

If your parents were divorced, you may become anxious as you approach the adult age at which they were separated. When our parents divorce, there is an underlying adult fear of intimacy because permanency of marriage is not assumed based upon our personal experience. Get individual or marital counseling for yourself and your spouse if this occurs.

Secrets about Santa and the Tooth Fairy — oops, I hope I didn't just give something away — are appropriate and fun. Secrets kept under threat, guilt, coercion, or the subtle "just between us" are never healthy even in the name of privacy or to protect someone's reputation in the family — no matter how much we love them.

Don't Tell Anyone

Steve was eleven when his school counselor said he appeared depressed: he had low energy, lost interest in activities he previously enjoyed, was quick to cry or argue, and seldom finished his lunch. He had just found out that his father, whom he loved, was actually his stepfather. It would take awhile to rebuild his trust in his parents and in his world in general. His mother had planned to tell him the truth *someday.*

Janet told her doctor she never confides in her mother anymore. Janet was molested by an uncle a few years before but her mother had told her to forget the incident since it happened so long ago. "Besides, it would just be your word against his."

Dave tugs at his lip exactly four times before eating. He believes that this ritual protects him against various potential catastrophes. At age 14, he realizes that this compulsion is irrational but he gets anxious when he tries to stop the habit. Twice he has seen his father angrily hitting his mother, but was told they were "only playing" when he asks them about it. They tell him not to be so nervous, but anxiety is natural when you cannot trust your own perceptions.

Family secrets make children lose trust, harbor resentment, and doubt themselves: they cause childhood anxiety and depression. Full repair of emotional and interpersonal damage is difficult when there are secrets about abuse and neglect. Keeping family secrets to protect the children is hardly protection at all. Seek professional help if you have questions as a parent and/or as a victim.

*****

As parents, the best way to teach humility and courage is by the modeling of our own behavior. Sharing your errors with your children actually helps them appreciate and copy your strengths. And when you share your failings, instead of getting the insults and humiliation you fear you will get, you will almost always find that it is healthy support and and understanding that you receive. Remember that secrets held inside are not healthy for any of us. If you are confused about the difference between privacy and secrets about incidents in your past, contact a mental health professional.

Here is yet another, albeit quick, reminder that attacking problems earlier instead of later is the smartest and least costly route to take. It is better to learn early that there is not a significant cause for concern than to realize later that you have waited too long.

Don't Ignore It

Ignoring problem behavior, such as a tantrum, is often the best course of action because you are not giving attention to negative and manipulating behavior by your child. But when there is an ongoing problem such as destructive or abusive behavior, ongoing or excessive anger, hyperactivity, depression, inability of one parent to compromise, alcoholism or drug abuse, or tantrums by your spouse — it cannot be ignored.

Healthy families have greater ability to confront issues as they arise. If one person in the family (child or adult) feels that a problem exists, then have it discussed among the people it effects directly. If the issue is felt to influence everyone in the home, either call a family meeting or make a parental decision that will be reevaluated in the near future. (See the chapter on Roundtable Discussions for guidelines on family meetings.)

Do not wait for the problem to disappear or attempt to make it do so — it may eventually destroy the health of your home. There is an advertisement in which a wrecking ball keeps crashing through the walls of a home, but all the family members continue their chores as if the demolition were not happening. This graphic description of ignored family problems is accurate regardless of the problem. Mental health — and illness — is contagious.

Be convinced that *your concerns are not trivial.* When you sense an ongoing problem, do not ignore it.

*****

There are times when a parent is convinced that there is (or is not a problem). If your first consult does not confirm your assessment, get a second reliable opinion. If both expert conclusions concur, accept your findings. If the two consultants disagree, get a third. Go with the majority decision.

SECTION 4.
INTRODUCTION TO CAROLINE

Caroline is a nine-year-old hesitant and unhappy girl. During the next five chapters, we will follow Caroline and her parents through the counseling process. Much like the Normals, Caroline's family is basically healthy and occasionally runs into snags. Caroline and her parents made much progress and all deserve credit for their improvement. Caroline, of course, is fictional, although I have counselled many Carolines of both sexes over the years. And the vast majority of them have left as happily as Caroline did.

Caroline is a sweetheart according to almost any teacher, aunt, uncle, neighbor, and parents of her friends. Up close, our own children seldom appear so ideal or thoroughly angelic because we live with them. Equally, when we slow down to peek at them or play with them on vacation, there are no children more precious than our own. Because we are so close to our children, sometimes their minor, human flaws become glaring. Sometimes we panic and rush in to fix these perceived flaws for the best of parental reasons like Hal and Sal Normal did. Sometimes a child's spot of weakness resembles a huge button of our own needing to be erased. Caroline represents one of these "sometimes."

Cautious Caroline: The First Session

Caroline usually gives one-word answers to her mother, often prefers playing alone. Her teacher says Caroline is very knowledgeable for her age although she is quiet in class. Both of her parents are energetic, with high expectations of themselves at work, in parenting Caroline, and in recreation. They are disappointed that Caroline shows little interest in competitive sports. "She just draws animals and writes stories in her room or plays house with her friends," her mother told me. Her parents wanted a more assertive and ambitious, if not aggressive, child in preparation for an adult life in what they emphasized was a mostly competitive world.

I began the first session with Caroline and her parents together. I faced Caroline first. "I will be asking you some nosey questions. You do not have to answer a nosey question if you do not want to. Further, when you and your parents have different answers to a question, that is okay with me. I assume everyone is telling the truth as they see it." As an example of my "equal truths" belief, I explained how two ideal birthday party plans could be made for Caroline's next birthday as an exaggeration. I tell how the parents' ideal party would probably allow for a few friends, cake, and burgers and fries, and soda for all at the bowling alley. That would be their truth. Easy. Fun. And no mess in

the house to clean up afterward. (Sounds almost perfect to me, come to think of it.) Caroline, and most children turning ten, would probably opt for most of their same-sex classmates to spend the night in the basement with five PG-13 videos, no bedtime, pizza delivery at 8:00 PM and an ice cream truck in the driveway at midnight. The parents do all the cleaning. Oh, and McDonald's breakfast for everyone at six the following morning. My goal in this example was to let Caroline and her parents know that I accept both viewpoints as equally valid. Neither party perspective is wrong.

"What school do you go to?" I asked. Caroline twirled her hair, looked around the room, and did not answer, mostly out of insecurity. I doubted she was the defiant type, although, I have to admit I occasionally get fooled.

"Answer him," her mother prodded sternly but lovingly.

"And what grade are you in?" I continued despite not getting an answer to my first query.

"Leave your hair alone and answer the question." Her father was speaking and getting annoyed. Then he turned to me. "Mr. Herz, we cannot have Caroline going through life so passively. What can we do? We have offered her incentives, rewards, and contracts to try some sports — just to try — all to no avail."

"Well," I began, realizing immediately, but too late, that my next comment would be more offensive than necessary. Treating people with respect is of utmost importance to me in and out of my office. I was not happy that I was manipulating a strong response, but felt it a bit needed to stop the parents focus on Caroline's imperfections. "Perhaps you could trade Caroline for a daughter you could find more lovable." I apologized for that line later on.

"Mr. Herz! Her mother and I love Caroline very much! We love her affection and her generosity. My wife still looks forward to reading to her at bedtime. Caroline and I have pancakes together every Sunday morning at our special restaurant." He winked at Caroline and she gave a solid grin in return.

All parents become disconcerted and discontented *with certain characteristics* of their children as well as with those of with each other. *None of us is perfect to ourselves either, much less to someone else.* However, Caroline's parents were attempting to change Caroline into someone she was not. Caroline's response to her parents disapproval was to close a number of her emotional boundaries to them, creating a play world where she could be who she wanted to be. We all have a need for such magical places, but to spend too much time there is to hide from life. *We parents need to prod our children* to try new activities. However, *we seldom need to force* participation to the point at where it becomes a battle. Try a different avenue or bring up the idea in another year when this happens.

"Caroline is acting codependently with you. She perceives her success and failure as being out of her control. She feels her goals are set by others and as a result has low insight into what goals she wants for herself. She knows more about the world and about other people than she knows about herself. She spends her energy trying to figure out what others want to hear before she answers. She has little confidence aside from learning rote facts to gain your approval. Much of her playing alone is to avoid discomfort."

I explained about keeping About Me Books for all three of them. Caroline would be initially skeptical of her parents' changes. I did not feel that her parents would be more accepting of Caroline just yet. Having patience would not came easily in their family. There was something underlying all this family pressure we still had not uncovered.

*****

Although Caroline did not need it since she was not a defiant child, there is another part of my guidelines I usually present along with "equal truths" when I sense unresolved parent-child battles for power in the family. I look at the parents and tell them *that children have rights to fairness, praise, and rewards as well as to appropriate consequences, and that I will help the children get this.* I know the children are listening carefully when I say this. Then, before the children can gloat too much, I turn to them and explain *the childhood need for authority* and my understanding that their parents have insight by virtue of their experience in life. I sum up by telling the youngsters, "Your parents need to be in charge. *And I will help them achieve this* if you start acting like the boss." By then, both the parents and children understand that I am aware of their roles and needs and that I will not take sides but will help their family run more smoothly, including arranging appropriate parent-child lines of command when needed.

We need to be patient when establishing trust with someone who is in emotional pain, allowing her to have control at least in the therapy office. Caroline needed patience and encouragement in order to say what she needed for emotional comfort. She was allowed to make her own choices and to do so at her own pace during our sessions — having control of herself was a new experience for her. Such freedom is seldom possible in life for children, but it can exist during the therapy session when that is the course of treatment necessary for progress.

Cautious Caroline: Fear Of Failure

Caroline arrived for the second session which I often spend one-to-one with the child in order to establish a relationship away from the parents. She showed no fear, excitement, or hesitation in leaving her mother but followed me dutifully down the hall as I had asked. She reminded me of Jeffrey who we met in chapter one.

I sat on the floor next to the toy shelf waiting for her to join me as most kids do. Caroline sat on the couch, behind a pillow, as if hoping to be invisible. I picked up a small stuffed bear and said to the bear, "You look shy and unhappy." I gently tossed the bear on the couch near Caroline. "How does Teddy look to you?" I asked quietly.

She leaned over to the bear slowly and placed it, unemotionally, on her lap. I spoke again. "When I am scared or sad I like a warm lap to sit on, too. Who takes care of you when you are unhappy?"

Caroline gave me the names of her sitter and her grandfather as favorite sources of nurturing before mentioning her parents. She reminded me of a worn Raggedy Ann doll. I used a hand puppet to talk to Caroline's bear, but she stayed cautious and distant. She would not risk revealing any part of herself about which I could disapprove. She would prefer that I asked questions that are knowledge-based as commonly found in school. When you are right, you are right. However, I was asking *open-ended questions where the answers are personal opinions — there are no wrong answers.*

She conversed using the bear to talk to the puppet, with more animation as the session progressed. However, she did not leave the safety of the couch until the end of the session and I respected the privacy of her hiding place.

Helping emotionally wounded children who sense conditional love is the basis of most of their relationships is not a rapid process. The rate of progress depends upon the length and depth of their insecurities, the existence of other healthy role models in their lives, and the optimism in their personalities. Caroline was anxious (cautious) and depressed (unemotional, passive, unhappy, and feeling helpless to please herself and others simultaneously). Children like Caroline, and adults who grew up in similar households, avoid the risk of being assertive and reaching out to others. Their underlying assumptions are that matters will only worsen. Such children lack adequate problem-solving skills and the necessary confidence to try to improve their condition. In general they do not trust themselves or others. Their low self-acceptance is a statement that instead of *making* mistakes like everyone else, they *are* mistakes.

In working with depressed and anxious children, I schedule the child, the parents, or the whole family depending on the results of the previous session. I made the next appointment just for Caroline again to continue building her trust in me and to help her improve her sense *of her own goals.* I would let her set the pace and distance according to her view of safety.

*****

Caroline's emotional predicament is not fully her parents' fault regardless of their positive or negative intentions. Nor are her successes fully the result of her parents' efforts. For better or for worse, *none of us have total control over how our children turn out.* This is because *we all have our own personalities and temperaments* influencing our emotions and behavior. Some of us are more active, assured, social, or aggressive. Others of us are typically more shy, cautious, and quiet. Part of Caroline's caution is just Caroline being Caroline. Our temperaments are comparable to the strengths versus the weaknesses of ADHD discussed before. We want to help our children (and ourselves) expand the strengths of their personalities and find the niches in which they will perform most successfully and comfortably.

Sometimes our reactions to our childhoods stay with us as hidden scars that influence our decisions as adults. We need to stop running every once in a while to assess the correctness of the decisions we automatically make. Should we continue on the same path, modify our direction, or chart an entirely new course? Be cautious in making alterations, but do not avoid making necessary modifications either. As another regular reminder for middle childhood, small alterations usually work best and last the longest.

Caroline's Parents and the Big Fear

I had spent two individual sessions with Caroline. She was slowly letting go of her cautiousness with me. However, her parents still became frustrated so quickly that the About Me Books were not helping much at home. I decided to meet with Caroline's parents by themselves. Admittedly, I found myself being somewhat frustrated with their resistance to letting go of their insistence that Caroline be more aggressive in life. Why were their efforts only superficial? *What were they afraid of?*

"When I was growing up," Caroline's mother began, "My parents seldom had the money for family vacations like most other kids had. My friends went to resorts while we slept in tents in state parks. I had to work my way through college and had little time for extra-curricular fun. I promised myself that my children would have the best and all they needed of it." There was a desperation in her voice that said Caroline would never be embarrassed by a lack of affluence. She pointed to her husband. "He had a similar childhood. We agreed before we were married that we were going to be first-rate parents."

Instead of feeling frustrated with them, I was now sympathizing with their fears of failure as providers. "You were embarrassed by your parents' financial failings, right?" They nodded. "And you were embarrassed by not being able to keep up with your more affluent peers, right?" They nodded again.

I paused. "Money is not the real issue for you although you believe it is. Both of you came from families where your parents were full of shame for being inadequate people in general, with finances being their focus of insecurity. Both of you inherited the Big Fear of being inadequate yourselves. You have a codependent problem of trying to fix your individual self-esteem by continually focusing on something outside yourselves. I am afraid that you cannot earn high enough incomes or gain high enough prestige to cure your emotional ailment. You have yourselves on a never-ending road to nowhere."

Caroline's father's eyes turned red. "I've always been afraid of that."

The Big Fear was out. Although they were highly successful in the outside world, they still felt like failures on the inside. I urged them to write at least one positive coaching comment daily in each other's About Me Book. Further, they were to take at least two minutes each day to just sit together and hold hands and to go out for dinner once a week – without Caroline. Fast food would be fine. Any more time away from work projects and chores would be too much of a change for now.

I summed up our session. "Remember, just try your best and eventually you will succeed. Take a minute to breathe to ten when you feel uncomfortable. The short breathing break will actually make you more efficient – it will not be a waste of time. Money is good to have. But you need to slow down to enjoy what you have earned. We all need to appreciate what we have more while we obsess about what we don't have less." As they walked out of the office I thought to myself, "Nice people."

*****

My emotional response to Caroline's parents was similar to their response to Caroline. The more I got to know about them personally, the more I found myself respecting and liking them. I find it *difficult to dislike or disrespect those whom I get close to* whether or not I agree with their views or lifestyle choices. Caring for people we become close to is true for how we view ourselves as well.

The best part of therapy —for the counselor and client alike — is seeing and feeling the progress. It is common for patients to eventually realize their growth as individuals, as family members, and as spouses. Often they wonder what they really feared about counseling at the outset.

Caroline - Session Six

Three sessions had been held with Caroline and two with her parents over the months since our initial meeting. Caroline was responding well to her individual therapy and to my coaching of her parents. This balanced approach is especially effective when the child's symptoms are the result of family problems that began generations ago.

"Look at this!" Caroline's father said with pride. He handed me a list of positive and negative memories he had about his own parents. His positive memory list was longer than the negative one — a healthy, yet realistic, balanced view.

Caroline's mother had written a similar list also and she spoke spoke next. "You told us we were going to talk about our shame and anger at our own parents as the blockage to being able to accept ourselves unconditionally. And you said that we could not accept Caroline more until we could accept ourselves better. So we came up with this activity on our own! We are going to put you out of a job yet!"

Their goals had been met. Caroline's family had improved in laughing in life, feeling pain and happiness, sharing their joys and fears openly, and stating both pride and anger directly and fairly. Those are the goals of therapy — to help people help themselves cope with their immediate problem and improve their skills at handling future problems.

Caroline had agreed to sign up for a soccer team that would begin next month. She and some of her friends had formed a cookie club and her mother took a turn being a baking supervisor, which included making sure the girls cleaned up the mess. Both parents worked a little less than when I first met them. Caroline's father was reading more fiction and spending less time with the *Wall Street Journal.* They had more balance in their lives.

Caroline's father then said, "I have the closing words for today. We do not need to have had the best parents in the world to have peace of mind ourselves. We just need to be able to look at our parents' lives, their struggles, the fears and hopes of their generation, and their personal strengths and weaknesses. Sometimes I forgot that my parents gave me much of my determination and caring as well as my fears. Thus, we have to look at our parents from all sides and be able to say to ourselves that, all things considered, my parents did the best parenting they could."

Caroline's mother took her husband's hand. "And we hope that Caroline will say that about us: that we did the best we could and that she loves us for that. And that she has more positive memories of us than negative ones."

I could not have said it better. And I was sure their hopes would come true.

*****

It seems that I usually learn as much from my clients as they learn from me.

A funny thing about counseling... It seems you have just said, "Hello, how can I help you?," and soon you are saying, "So long. And best of luck. Call me if you need a check-up someday."

Graduation Day

Caroline said she wanted cupcakes and french fries with gravy for the therapy graduation. It is important to have a closing to counseling that says the goals were met. The ceremony serves to review the progress gained and how it was accomplished, as well as a time for everyone to pat themselves and each other on the back. It is an event that marks the start of getting on with life without a therapist's guidance. And it is a time to say goodbye.

I made the cupcakes. The fries were the microwavable kind. I got a cup of gravy from a restaurant near my office. The fries and gravy were better than I thought they would be.

My closing thought for Caroline's family was that they should view counseling as a healthy option in life. We all need consultants occasionally. *Seeking a mental health consultant is a strength, not a weakness* — it says you accept your need to regain balance with humility.

As we stood in that awkward moment of farewell, Caroline gave me a hug and I shook her parents' hands warmly. As they turned to leave, her mother pivoted and took my hand again. Her eyes were red. She was about to say something when she noticed my eyes also revealed the sting of loss. "You, too?" she mused.

"Yes, sometimes, me too."

*****

It is important to set an annual ceremony to celebrate the efforts and growth your family makes. Have a planning meeting. Congratulate yourselves for the progress you achieve. *Do not be modest.*

SECTION 5.

INTRODUCTION TO DEVELOPMENT

So much of successful parenting is knowing what to expect from our children at different ages. What is normal behavior at one stage of development is either maturity or immaturity at other stages. What is cute at one time is rude a few years later. What is a good attention span at age seven may signify ADHD at age twelve. There are effective methods of discipline and motivation used one year that were inappropriate and unfair three years before that. Had I tossed the teddy bear to Caroline when she was twelve, she would have thrown it back in disgust or at least felt highly insulted that I would treat her as such a youngster. If I'd tossed the bear at a four-year-old my action in a first individual session might have been misunderstood or even frightening especially without mom or dad being present.

The middle childhood years have their own flavor. The children are no longer the little kids of kindergarten. Nor are they ready for the push toward the independence of high school. If you have a middle childhood child you know she is not just spending her years waiting to be a teenager. Middle childhood is a time to develop competencies, grow to love peer relationships, and consider autonomy while still respecting and loving family life for the most part. The world of school and organized activities are as central to her universe as her home world is. Middle childhood is a time to help your child learn tasks but is not a time to be overbearing. Your supervision and guidance are certainly needed and often requested. You help your child find solutions now more than give answers. This is a time of great energy and an expanding world for your child.

Children learn about life by exploring, observing, questioning — and most frustrating to their parents — by testing your rules and limits. You may notice that middle childhood temperaments seem to shift between more compliant years and more defiant years. Your observations are correct. Your goal is to stay consistent in the face of their inconsistency. Good luck! When their testing gets near your emergency button levels, breathe to ten and consider the age-appropriateness of their behavior and attitude. Finally, choose the intervention of your choice according to your style of parenting and your child's patterns of handling situations. Soon you will be approaching serenity, sanity and mutual respect.

This developmental section covers seven of ten stages in life: infancy, toddlerhood, preschool, primary grades, middle childhood (which gets detailed year-by-year coverage), teen years (two stages of the years 13-15 and 16-18 lumped into one in this book) and adulthood which spans the years of bearing children up to the time when most of us have had the majority of our children complete the middle childhood years. Middle age — as in ages 45-65, not the days of knights and castles – and the elder years are not covered. I describe the years prior to middle childhood to explain what development has usually been achieved by now or to see what healthy development has been missed so you can prepare yourself and your children to make up for lost time or for serious and chronic parenting flaws. If the descriptions of adulthood sound more advanced than you feel you are, re-read the chapter on adolescence to see where you got stuck. You cannot effectively guide your children through the stages you have not completed yourself. Immature parents are destined to beget emotionally unhealthy children no matter how loving and they are. Similarly, if ADHD describes you, the parent, this problem needs to be dealt with in order for your children to receive consistent and appropriate parenting.

A common flaw in parenting, especially when we are annoyed with our children's actions, is using the phrase, "When I was your age...." Our memories are colored by our opinions, feelings, and our limited ability to see all sides of a situation when we are children (or at any age for that matter). These decades-old recollections are never a good basis for deciding what is age - appropriate in terms of your children's behavior. Of course, it is fun to give those lectures to our kids and to share those recollections with them. Just do not insist on your accuracy as though it were historic fact.

...And It's Normal

This is a true story about letting a child's normal-for-his-age behavior be treated as just that: *normal behavior.* When we parents understand what is developmentally appropriate, especially when we do not like what our child is doing at the moment, we can take our deep breaths and tell ourselves "and it's normal." That way we, *yes we*, do not overreact. We can reset our perspective about the situation by asking ourselves what the objective of *our behavior* is about. These priority checks help us avoid damaging our children or our relationships with them.

...The January air was cold and crisp. The sky was deep blue. The snow had created a flawless white carpet on the lawn at least six inches high. Best of all for my third-grade son, school was closed. I had taken the morning off from office paperwork so that he and I could go sledding. Now, as late morning approached, we had to head for the local slope soon or forgo the adventure. It was now or never, for today that is. Worse, although the sled was calling, so was a TV show he just *had* to see...

As an adult who loves winter, there was no dilemma for

me. To my young son, *who happened to think like a child,* there were dual attractions of equal import. And, although I explained that time continued to pass while he was deciding — a nice way of saying, "We haven't got all day, kid!" — the boy remained stuck. Finally, he decided to go for the snow. We had a great time, albeit not the whole morning full of fun I'd imaged when I first suggested sledding the hills.

Had I insisted on the sledding earlier, we might have had many tears and worse indecision, maybe never getting into the white stuff at all. (And maybe the tears would have dried quickly and a winter-funtime-with-hot-chocolate-and-all might have taken place.) I'll never know for certain. With different children, different approaches work better than others. In addition, what works for one parent *does not necessarily work for the spouse* dealing with the same child.

* * * * *

... Moral... When you feel like your child is "acting like a child," that is *probably the way he should be acting.* When in doubt, consider child development. Reset your buttons as needed. You do not have to respond immediately, unless there really is an emergency.

In order to develop healthy self-esteem, a child needs to hear certain messages at each stage regarding her identity and how she should explore her physical and social world. These messages, and the parental actions that must accompany them, represent love, mutual respect, and appropriate boundaries. Since we are the parents, we better look at our own developmental stage —adulthood — first. This way we can differentiate (1) when we wish we were still a child, being a child at heart, (2) how to play with our children while retaining our parental role, and (3) when we are acting like children, having lost our adult role for the time being. All three are normal conditions, although the third must be kept to a minimum when the children are present or within earshot.

Adulthood

In adulthood, our roles of child to our own parents, of parent, spouse, and individual merge. Like our children, we all have our own goals list that needs to be filled. However, as confident adults, we need not depend upon our own parents, spouses, peers, or supervisors as our primary sources of praise. (If you are not confident and did not receive the various health messages in your own childhood, you may require therapeutic assistance in re-parenting yourself.) In order to be effective parents we need to be healthy adults. And vice versa.

In addition to immediate family life, this stage includes occupation, possible further education, concerns with our aging parents, financial plans for the future, and the *ongoing task of accepting the natural limitations* of age and reality. The basic messages — most of which we will tell ourselves — are:

1. "You are productive and creative." You can work and enjoy life in balance and feel satisfied in your efforts and successes at work, play, and home.

2. "You can trust your gut to lead you." Too often, we ignore our intuitive guide and listen only to friends, co-workers, books, and other "experts." In reality, our inner feelings will usually decide for us regardless of our level of intelligence or education.

3. "You are good enough as you are." You can accept that you are not perfect in any aspect of life. You can endorse yourself for your efforts and choices so far. You can share *responsibility for fault and success* with others involved in your life.

4. "You can be both independent and interdependent with others at work and home." You can enjoy time alone and in social activity as you need to. You can say "yes or no or *I will think about it"* as needed with minimal negative guilt. You can ask for whatever you need or want: the response may be "no" but otherwise your silent request is left to complete chance.

5. "You can take care of yourself." Through your life experiences and ability to gain perspective, you realize that you are neither the center of the universe nor a mere orbiting satellite. You can do the job alone, get help, or call experts into your life as necessary,

6. "You can still play." And you need to. You can play alone or with others both spontaneously and in organized activities. You can try new methods of play without worry that your past adolescent crowd approves.

7. "Keep growing." Do not stay stagnant when boredom continues. Keep learning whether in classes, activities, reading, hiking, or challenging yourself with hobbies. Unlike high school days, when a subject is not to your liking, you do not need to continue the class unless the classes are for credit since grades only count at school and at work. And even then, keep a perspective about the need to get perfect scores.

8. "You can reevaluate your plans, goals, and dreams." How can we know at age 20 what we want to be doing at age 40? How can we really know, before our first child, what life will be like with all four of the kids we originally planned to have? Our plans must not be more than a flexible guide. You can change your mind and likes.

9. "I am chronically lovable." If you were your own peer, I hope you would choose yourself as a friend.

10. "I am fair to myself and others." I can make compromises in both my demands of, and in disagreements with, others. And I will accept those compromises and losses as they occur, grieve as needed, and then get on with my life.

*****

Adulthood, like every stage of life, is a period of learning, exploring, experiencing, and challenge. Do not expect to have all the answers at any given time or you will be sadly disappointed with yourself. In other words, *try your best* at all you do with large doses of *humor and humility* in your pocket at all times. For those times when you are making children, or just practicing, you my not have pockets, so be sure to keep your humor and humility close by on the nightstand.

Talk about a change in our lives! Talk about no advanced training! When your first child comes along, the challenge and responsibility is both frightening and exhilarating. Your hopes and fears are nearly overwhelming. The love and pride can feel barely bearable.

Earliest Messages: Infancy

I view human development in ten stages, eight of which are covered in this book: Infancy, Toddlerhood, Reasoning, Preschool, Big Kids, Middle Childhood, Independence, and Adulthood. The last two stages, Middle Age and Aging, will not be discussed.

The infancy stage opens when our parental energy and hopes are usually at an optimistic peak. Sometimes, depending upon how our lives are going, we may feel more burdened with our infant than excited. As we must learn to tell our children (and ourselves), *any feeling* we have is acceptable. When we feel burdened by having children, we do not need to add negative guilt to it. Especially with our first child, we must relax our perfectionistic expectations: *parenthood is a family expedition* into the partly-known — at best.

Below are the five messages your infant needs to hear and feel from her parents between birth and the time she walks. This stage sets the *foundation* for emotional health in later stages. It is an error to ignore your child's needs with the excuse that "she's only a baby." She needs these messages delivered from both parents. Begin the two-parent teamwork quest for balance as early as possible when your family has two parents.

1. "I, your parent, am glad I have you and accept you just the way you are." A child cannot accept

herself, with both her strengths and weaknesses, if her parents do not accept her.

2. "I will be here when you call. I will respond to your cry and will listen for your gurgles, too." Consistency in communication has to exist in your relationship so that she can see the world as a safe and trustworthy place for the most part. It says you respect her needs as she defines them. *You won't spoil her at this age.*

3. "My love is unconditional." You love her just the way she is and generally enjoy time with her, although you will feel frustrated when she cries just when you need peace and quiet the most.

4. "You be you, and I'll be me. And we will be a team, too." You will enjoy your time together singing, playing, and learning yet both of you need to have your own identities and times alone. Your child cannot make you happy or miserable in life — only you and luck are responsible for that. *Flexible boundaries* are necessary for healthy family living.

5. "I am an able and balanced parent and you are perfect enough, too. We both learn by trying our best."

*****

Most years prior to adolescence have shifts in attitude and or exuberance from year to year. Some years are easier for parents, some easier for children, some smooth for both. And some years, you guessed it, may require United Nations troops stationed right in the living room. Enjoy infancy. The troops of experience are on alert in the near distance. The toddlers are coming and you cannot stop them!

I hope I did not scare you into throwing this book away when I ended the last chapter saying, "the toddlers are coming." They are coming, but "the terrible twos" are not terrible. In fact, they are fascinating! Your language centers on the word "no" as they begin to walk upright. As upwardly and mobile little citizens, they can see and touch all sorts of things previously out of sight, out of reach, and out of grasp. This new world of theirs is fantastic to them. And what do we adults do? We put all this great stuff almost in reach, tantalizing them, and then yell "No!" just as they almost grab some golden object. Who can blame them for being contrary in attitude and yelling "no" right back at us? Life for a toddler is like an "everything's free" day at the mall but mall cop keeps saying, "You can't have that, don't touch that, leave that alone." Oh the opportunities. Oh, the frustration. For our purposes, two-and three-year-olds are together in this chapter.

Toddlers: On The Brink Of Reasoning

Historically, the Age Of Reason took place a number of centuries ago. Developmentally, it begins a bit after age one and lasts almost two years. During this stage, the child learns to think for himself — but do not expect any real sense of judgment. His childhood reasoning has its own brand of logic, which, to him, is infinitely more sensible than yours. A number of developmental experts understandably refer to this stage as a first adolescence, although you do have more leverage now than you will in the ten-plus years when the real adolescence hits. "Because I wanted to" makes perfect sense to him although — never fear —he will start to understand that feelings do not necessarily justify actions before this stage is over. Note, I said *start to understand.* He is just beginning to accept that he is not the center of the universe, and that his reasons are not the only valid reasons. Again, just starting. Keep your expectations low.

He is not physically ready to start toilet training prior to two and same children are not ready until closer to three. To force him into toilet training before he has the muscular readiness tends to create *mutual embarrassment* and defeat. Forcing tasks before he is capable of succeeding will result in shame and frustration for parent and child alike.

Encourage the use of feedback to be sure he understands you. Repeat what he says to you to model and encourage accuracy in communication. The emotional messages he needs to hear now, *in addition to the ones he heard in infancy,* are:

1. "Follow your natural curiosity." He needs your protection from injury and your provision of safe ways to learn about his world. You realize he uses all of his senses to explore life — especially his hands and mouth (which does not mean he will try a taste your avocado ice cream). Childproof the house by crawling around to see the house as he does. Put childproof locks anywhere he should not be. Do not let him fall hard in hopes that he will learn "the hard way" not to disobey you — he is *not capable of learning from errors* yet. In addition, some errors can be dangerous or even fatal.

2. "You can ask me anything. Anything." This message conveys that he can inquire about any subject: sex, money, real reality, *and his reality.* He does not need to figure out whether or not his question is valid to you at any stage. There are no stupid questions now. (In theory there are never stupid questions, unless he is between

ages nine and twelve when kids frequently love to ask clearly ridiculous questions purely to pester and test your self-control.) There is no blame for misunderstandings since clear communication is a shared responsibility. He needs a model of how to solve problems that says *"we* will find solutions together."

3. "You are an amazing creature who is fun to watch grow up." Did I mention that he can also be an exasperating little creature? His insights and approaches to learning are wonderful to observe and his intellectual growth will take place naturally for the most part especially with your guidance and the provision of challenges and surprises. *Jump right in.* But do not force learning or readiness in hopes of creating a superchild or getting a head start on brilliance or athletic skills. *Do* read often to him. Play with him regularly.

4. You already know this one: "Anger is an OK feeling." He needs to hear this and have you model it for him as well. Tell him about the things in your life that annoy you but resist telling him how you handled them for now since *feelings*, not solutions and morals, are the focus here.

5. "I love you when you are in motion and when you are at rest." Of course, his choice for motion will sometimes come when you have hoped he was at rest. The telephone hold-button was probably created out of necessity by the parent of a toddler.

6. "You can test me — I will still love you." Part of satisfying curiosity and seeking stability results

in his testing the limits you have just set. *The scientist in him wants to know how we adults work.* (Sometimes I wish *I* knew how we adults work!) Thus, he has to probe and poke to see how we respond. For better or worse, you are one of his prime laboratories.

7. "You can ask for help and I will help you as best as I can." This does not mean you can always help out immediately, but it means you understand his request as legitimate and important to him. His task may seem trivial to you, but it is important to him.

8. "You can go your own way and I will still be here for you." Of course, he will hopefully not go too far, but you are telling him he is free to have his own identity, not having to stay by your side all the time. You are available for him to share his treasures and victories as well as his exhaustion, frustration, and his sudden requests for hugs and kisses. This message encourages healthy boundaries in his search for identity. (In a physical sense of exploration, a child with ADHD may actually stray too far due to his difficulty following directions plus and due to having a limited sense of danger, distance, and elapsed time. If your child has ADHD, you may already notice this problem. Childproof his physical boundaries as needed for his safety — which is *not the same* as limiting him merely to make your day easier.

*****

And there is a message for adults to help us reset our own emergency buttons: "My toddler's striving to think for himself — which often means 'No, Mom, I do not want to do what you want me to do' — and this stubbornness of his is *not to be taken personally* by me, the parent." His first stabs at having an identity is to state that he is different from you. Give quick doses of affection ten seconds after the tantrum is over. You understand that your youngster was only in *confusion mode,* not attack mode. Clearly nothing personal. He is trying to form his early sense of *who he is.*

The ages of approximately three-and-a-half through six are the first years aimed at autonomy. She just got a basic idea of being a person in her own right. Now she wants to go out in the world, her world, which means taking on the neighborhood and the playground on her own. She wants to show off her new personhood to local peers with their new personhoods. Of course, you are not to let her go so far away that she cannot get to you immediately —which is not the same as expecting her to come home the moment you call.

I'm Me!

Ages three to the beginning of kindergarten (at about age five) are based on a search for identity. Identity includes knowing how strong she is in terms of getting her physical, emotional, social and curiosity needs met. The power struggles of the "terrible twos" will recur frequently. And, if you thought she had energy at two, hold on tight. She needs encouragement to find her own sense of being with a solid dose of balanced expectations and limitations from you, too. When in doubt, lean toward encouragement, patience, and understanding. Ask her many questions about her world and enjoy hearing some "facts" you never learned in school. Do not insist that she is wrong when her facts of living are different from yours. As to discipline, her reasoning is ever sharper and she will demand that you give proof about her wrongdoings. However, like Hal Normal, you can be *neither judge nor jury* and you can apologize if you are later found wrong. Without doubt, she will have fun pretending, too. Below are the necessary parent messages for children at this stage. As with other stages, these new messages are built upon the previous ones and continue to show no-strings-attached love.

1. "Find out who you are and be *proud of your similarities and differences from me.*" Encourage her to establish and explore other relationships, too.

2. "You are as powerful as you need to be for your age." She can ask for help without being weak. *In fact, seeking necessary assistance is a sign of strength at any age.* Only give as much help as she asked for or your controlling of her issue will result in resentment, a sense of helplessness to handle the parts of her own problems, and she may become less likely to seek your help in the future.

3. "You can have any feelings and opinions and you can share them with me when you want." This says that you will be her sounding board no matter what the topic. This is easier said than done, as is most of parenting.

4. "You are the child: I am the parent." These roles are important for her security and safety. She cannot safely explore the world of relationships if there is insufficient consistency behind her. This message also says you will not let her hurt herself or let her get hurt — and when there are hurts, you will protect her from further pain as best you can.

*****

Message four from the last chapter serves as a connection to the next stage, middle childhood — where your role and you will be challenged more. Challenge is neither good nor bad, but merely signifies a time of growth for all involved. Before the end of first grade, somewhere before his seventh birthday, this stage usually shifts in a subtle manner from the generally cooperative kindergartner into the "I'll call you later, mom/dad. You don't need to call me" almost second-grader. He is not saying this with impudence, but rather with a sense of I-can-take-care-of-myself. In some of the upcoming more defiant, upheaval years, you may be breathing to ten at least twice daily. During the smoother years you may only be breathing to gain your calm twice a week. It may be too late, but you may want to space your pregnancies so that all of your children hit those easier years at the same time. Of course, if you do manage this feat, your children's coinciding chaos years could be unbearable for you!

The messages of middle childhood will be explained along with an in-depth, year-by-year explanation of physical, social, emotional, and family aspects of development. As explained previously in "And It's Normal," the more you know about child development the more smoothly you will roll with your child's ups and downs.

Middle Childhood —Ages 7 Through 12

Middle childhood is the stage of finding balance. The child knows who he is as an individual (for now) although the re-identification of adolescence is not far off. Most of his life is about school, with the emphasis of school learning moving from exploring issues to looking up the "right" answer (Luckily, the trend in education today is toward emphasizing more experiential, hands-on, learning.) He is learning about responsibility in studying, homework, saving allowance, doing chores, and being fair to others. His friends, who are mostly of the same sex, become more important than you — or so it seems at times. He is amazed at how much you *don't* know. You are amazed at how much he does *and* does not know. This increasingly independent "tough guy" is still a kid in full need of your love, guidance, support, and modeling, although he increasingly asks for them in the strangest and often least direct ways. Being able to make his own breakfast, ride a bike to school or to the store, and mow lawns to support his candy habit is not real independence, although *to him it is.*

The general parent role is that of helper and structurer. You also are finding a balance between stepping back, being available, and taking charge to *limit his decisions when he is irresponsible.* (Remember, of course, to give him second, third, and fourth chances to show he can be more responsible.) The following messages cover the *entire* middle childhood stage, although there will be periodic adjustments by both you and your child.

1. "I will let you do what you can without my interference.But I will also be here when you need me." This speaks to the balance of independence and his need to still have adults make decisions for him. His irresponsibility is often his way of asking for help, although he will furiously deny it. Most often, the lack of responsibility is just your child *acting his age.*

2. "I will give you all the choices and decisions you can handle — no more and no less." This allows him to practice decision-making in the safety of your guidance as well as to learn how to set priorities about which goals to seek and try to achieve.

3. "I will help you learn from your mistakes and help you feel proud of how you learn from them." Self-acceptance includes acknowledging strengths and weaknesses with humility.

4. "I will help you learn the rules of life and help you challenge the ones you feel are unfair." You show him you love and respect him, whether or not you agree with his views.

5. "I will help you learn perspective in life." There are pros and cons of every decision about which he will need ongoing reminders. Humor is a large part of perspective, and although you heard most of his jokes when you were his age, you understand that this is another aspect of development. Some years he will have more humor and flexibility to see a wider perspective of his place in the world than other years.

*****

A year-by-year description of normal development follows. Each child will vary from the norm in his own way — as he should.Further, your child may be ahead in some areas and behind in others. Oldest children in the family, especially if there has been a divorce or death of a parent, are usually ahead in responsibility but commonly behind emotionally and low in self-awareness. The youngest children are commonly less responsible with immaturity increased when family traumas occur. And each child has his own personality — his unique personal touch to approaching life's tasks and offering surprises to you and to himself in reacting to the stresses of both success and failure.

Ten Areas Of Development

For each of the ages 7 to 12, there will be a separate chapter. There will be ten categories to watch for at each age.Remember that each child will be more advanced in some areas than in others. Certainly, physical development has a wide range of difference from child to child, especially in the years nine to twelve. Further, a child who is ahead, for example, in physical coordination at age eight, may be average at age ten. He may be behind or ahead again by age twelve. Do not be worried as long as the *general development is on target and there are no glaring deficits.* Being far ahead of peers in any particular field separates them from others for better or for worse. There are many fine books that provide greater depth in child development if you need more information. See the bibliography at the end of this book or consult your local bookseller or librarian.

Here are the ten areas of development to be discussed for each year of middle childhood in this section:

1. *Approach to Life* explores whether or not a particular year is mostly a year of inward focus and introspection marked by longer periods of withdrawal and reflection. These are years of calm growth beneath the surface usually accompanied by lower general energy. Other years, which usually alternate with the inward years, see more aggression in terms of vast energy in attacking life to the point which you may wonder if your child is hyperactive. Remind yourself that hyperactivity does not usually appear one year at a time, although there are factors which effect the intensity of ADHD,

anxiety, and, depression which may shift from one year to another such as specific teachers and the peer combinations in his classes.

2. *Identity* discusses how he views who he is and how he fits in with others and with the world in general. This is both a personal and spiritual question depending upon how deep a thinker he is. Our adult modeling helps our children define what it means "to be a man" and "to be a woman."

3. *Physical Development* describes body changes including sexual maturation, food appetite, energy levels, coordination, growth in height and weight, and his interest in whether others are changing in any particular ways.

4. *Emotional Reactions* illuminates the stability of his feelings and how his moods are generally displayed. More aggressive growth years tend to have lower patience and greater impulsivity. The quieter years tend to have more tears and worries.

5. *Home Life* shows how he feels about being home and whether he tends to hide in his room or be out with you. It explains, in other words, his level of comfort with family activities.

6. *Parents* portrays his responses to, and the seeking of, time with you. Some years he will seek you primarily for love and security. Other years he will want to argue, either due to moodiness or because his peers are argumentative. *He is seeking practice from you* — someone who might send him to his room or ground him for two days for being rude, but will *not* withdraw their love for him. In other words,

the good news is that he trusts and needs you. The bad news is that he feels safe enough to practice his most obnoxious behavior on you.

7. *Siblings* describes how he displays his pride in his brothers and sisters versus the times when he can barely stand to be in the same house with them. Often there are increased sibling problems with blended families as it is normal for each original family group of children to protect their own parent and to keep their prior identity and way of living.

8. *Peers* covers the slow (?) shift in middle childhood from peers-as-playmates to the time when friends eventually become the center of his life and the major influence on his ideas. At age eight you can choose his clothing for him. By age eleven, you don't know fashion any better than an old man with white shorts, black socks, and bright red cowboy hat. This is true even if you are a designer of teenage apparel. This topic also includes illustrations of how he solves differences with his peers and reaches compromises with them.

9. *School Life* encompasses much of his social life and is the center of his academic learning. His ability to think evolves from the basic memorizing of facts to being able to perform research and form complex conclusions.

10. *Other Development* covers intelligence, expressions, language, humor, and other subjects that are commonly of particular interest for a specific year.

Age 7 — Mostly Second Grade

Approach To Life. This is a mostly serious year but active at the same time. Ms. Seven is busy and persistent in investigating her world, which usually consists of her neighborhood. She is cautious about straying too far from home and school although some children are certainly more adventurous than others. She is frequently out of balance and thus is often self-absorbed in trying to make sense of herself and those around her. At seven, girls and boys are basically similar in most aspects of life, although girls are more likely to have dolls and the themes of play usually involve happy endings for all while boys are leaning toward themes of battle in which the endings tend to include victory for one side over the other. Both may still sleep with a menagerie of stuffed animals.

Identity. She knows she is no longer a kindergartner/first grader but she is not sure of who she is much beyond that. Again, this is a mostly out-of-balance year wherein she defines herself by what she is not instead of what she is.

Physical Development. To be blunt, not much is going on. Sevens are fussy in eating — big deal. Her awareness of sexual differences is not a big concern and, aside from a mother or aunt, or teacher being pregnant, sex and development are not major issues this year.

Emotional Reactions. She is pretty stable this year, although often solitary in play. Any tension is usually observable though nail-biting, hair-tugging, eye-blinking, and so forth. She will not sit still to discuss feelings a lot, in part due to not having the vocabulary and the abstract understanding that talking about problems leads to comfort and solutions. Certainly, some sevens are more verbal than others.

Home Life. She is secure at home and not ready to

venture too far without at least an older sibling or older neighbor to take her out. Even then, she does not want to be too far from view of home without an adult. She cannot understand why teens would want to go the mall without their parents. She can do simple chores around the house, often willingly or voluntarily, but requires supervision in most cases. Chores are good habits to build under the category of, "We all help out because we all live here."

Parents. You are needed, often requested, and seen as a major playmate. Games and activities with you are sought. You still know almost everything in her eyes. Enjoy your expertise while you still have it.

Siblings. In this year of self-centeredness, her siblings are not of great interest. Of course, she can still be a lot of fun with her brothers and sisters as well as knowing how pester them. She is not usually in major competition with her siblings although her older sisters and brothers may feel that seven gets away with too much and complain with, "But, when I was her age..."

Peers. Friends at home and at school and favorite relatives are frequently "best friends" although seven is generally low in social initiative. If she continues to have habits such as thumb sucking and carrying a favorite stuffed animal, she will probably quit on her own this year, or at least quit in public where peers might see her. Some keep their favorite creatures around until age ten, with often girls playing and sleeping with them longer.

School Life. Seven is now in at least her second year of full day school and knows all the rules there. (Some sevens, however, may have started school late due to your decision to avoid her being one of the youngest in her class or due to a preschool teacher's comments or pre-kindergarten assessment showing she is not fully ready to start first grade. Such decisions are usually sensible and I recommend not rushing your child into a grade in which she will be struggling. At ages four, five, and six, it is better to wait a year.) Seven usually enjoys academic learning and is quite comfortable there. If fears of attending school arise, see the school counselor and re-read the chapter on anxiety. Her confidence at school will be low if she is affected by learning disabilities, ADHD, or reading deficits which may not become evident until second or third grade, especially if they are mild problems. *If your child is struggling in a number of academic areas, especially if she is also having social or attentional difficulties, the earlier that grades are repeated the easier it is for her, you, and her teachers.* At the same time, if your school suggests your daughter repeat a year, be sure the school experts can explain why and, equally important, what will be the *positive result* of such an action. Be certain all learning disabilities have been investigated. If there has been a recent parental death or divorce, and there are already other accompanying school problems, a year to catch one's breath may be positive. However, again, do not have your child repeat a year just because the school does not know what else to do. Repeating a grade is a type of educational surgery — when needed it can be a very good move. Just be sure it it the *best* move *of the options* available to you.

Other Development. Her artwork shows more detail than before. Her language includes words and concepts with more diversity than "always or never," and "best or worst," and "love or hate." Her sense of time is still weak but she knows the days, weeks, and months solidly by the end of the year. This helps in answering, "How long til Grandma comes?" Money is probably not a major issue since she does not consider her independence (as in, "I can buy what I want with my own money!") much yet. She will just ask you to buy it for her. Tell her "yes or no," including a quick reason why, but skip the lectures on not getting everything you want — you are teaching her that everytime the answer is no.

Age 8: Mostly Third Grade

Approach to Life. Age eight is a more energetic, more enthusiastic, more outgoing, and more social year for the most part. Compared to the previous year, eight is a year of more: more curiosity, more exploration, more activity, more daring, more courage. This could also mean less judgment and less attention fo detail and guidelines. He sounds more grown up at times. Santa, the Easter Bunny, and the Tooth Fairy commonly become unemployed this year. You, as parent, still have a job. Your praise and attention remain extremely important. He may belittle the compliments you give him as a ploy to have you heap on the acclaim even more. Don't disappoint him: heap away.

Identity. He has a stronger sense of who he is and where he is going at eight: "Out. I'm going out." He has some sense of what he wants to be when he grows up. He likes money more now since being out often means spending. He likes to be dramatic. At meals, there is less of, "I don't want to eat this" and more of, "Ugghh! What is this gross stuff!" Gently insist on manners since the message about rude behavior at the table is usually lost five-minutes later. He actually is more responsible and can get himself up and going in the morning. School days, however, will still require numerous reminders from you including, "Eat your breakfast, the bus will be here soon, don't forget your backpack and lunch money...and where is my kiss goodbye." He knows he is a boy (and she knows she is a girl). Personal appearance, grooming, and clothes often become more important at eight. In general, he likes himself this year.

Physical Development. Appetite is up again to support all the mental and physical activity and exploration. Manners may even be observed a bit more this year. Growth spurts are common in year eight. Health is quite good but scrapes and scratches increase with all his moving and exercise. Coordination and strength make large gains this year though visible musculature may not change much yet.

Emotional Reactions. Mr. Eight is more reasonable, curious, and interested in the hows of conception beyond sperm meets egg. He is also more interested in God, creation of the universe, and death. Due to his love for dramatics, he can be fussier and touchier and will undoubtedly let you know if you have offended him.

Home Life. Cooperation is generally good and completion of assigned tasks improves. Initiation of chores, however, is still quite weak. Expect him to need reminders.

Parents. The good news is eight is more open to adult reasoning than the year before. However, much of his testing of life *is aimed at Mom.* She gets the brunt of his anger and confusion. Equally, Mom is to be protected from harm, injury, and especially from nefarious siblings who might pester her when he is in his protect-Mom mood. If Dad is a custodial single parent, he gets the heavy doses of love and attack from the eight year-old. In two-parent families, Dad (or Stepdad) can coach Mom (or Step mom) since she usually gets the majority of strong emotions. (Of course each parent should be an equal coach for the other. It is just that in certain years, Mom will get more hassle from the children than others. Other years they will get equal amounts of flack.) Eight is a better observer now and will watch both (all) parents carefully for *any marital shows of affection, mutual respect, and the solving of arguments.*

Siblings. The bad news for siblings, especially younger ones, is that Eight has little use for them unless they are below age five and still often "cute." Older siblings, especially if four or more years ahead can be okay (or even better if they can drive). This pattern will continue through most of middle childhood.

Peers. He has stronger friendships this year. Because

eight's identity is more solid now, both his friends and non friends are more clearly identifiable. His closest friends will usually be boys. (This same pattern is seen with girls — their closest friendships are with other girls.) He likes to make deals and compromises with peers and parents. Following through on compromises *is not* his goal, which

can be frustrating to parents. Most of the peers understand that the *deal making itself is the goal.* Sexual relations consist mostly of mutually chasing one another with no real idea of what to do if the catch is made. Both sexes increase in the use of dirty words. He will often be quite critical of himself and of his peers, but this seldom lasts for very long. If there are religious, nationalistic, or racial overtones to his comments, *react quickly but with love:* remember that this behavior is about identity. Your goal is to calmly remind him of how much all of us are alike despite differences. His imagination is used in play although there is less pretending.Girls tend to enjoy putting on plays and cooking (which usually does not mean anything about cleaning up to them). Boys enjoy using tools (and, like the girls, seldom includes the practice of cleaning up). I believe that boys need to know how to cook (beyond heating macaroni in the microwave) and girls need to know how to use tools to increase their independence skills in life. Both enjoy sports, washing cars, and having lemonade stands to earn money.

School. He is still an enthusiastic student with a strong interest in learning. He respects his teacher and seeks his or her praise. His highlight of the day is catching the teacher in a mistake. Studying geography and the universe are appealing since his personal world is also expanding rapidly this year.

Other Development. Eight year-olds are basically honest. He wants to be seen as ethical and moral although he will still have difficulty accepting his part of the responsibility for problems and failures. Drawing and discussion skills both increase in detail and range of expression including frequent facial contortions to accompany his chatter. You, the parent, may find it difficult to not laugh at times when you might prefer to keep a serious look on your face although he is often not actually trying to be comically entertaining.

Heroes To The Rescue

Larchmont, New York, was a quiet suburban town in the 1950s. Fires were handled by the fire department. Crimes were solved by the police. But when real crises occurred, you could feel secure thanks to the Larchmont Rangers.

Louis and I, both aged 9, and a host of imaginary teammates saved victims, fought invaders, and handily beat the New York Knicks and Yankees with our amazing athletic feats. Our record was flawless.

We were the best of buddies and the Rangers were part of our play world in third and fourth grades. They helped us deal with the normal inner concerns of general competence, horrors in the news, fears of ghosts and the unknown, and doing well in school.

Often, we adults view our children's play as *"wasting time"* as opposed to realizing its importance in development and practice in coping with the world at large. Listen to your children at play, join them, without intruding, and help them role-play in solving their issues. Most play is rehearsal for possible conflicts and future incidents as the children anticipate these occurrences.

If you prove to be a capable and trusted participant, you just might be deputized a Ranger, too.

Age 9: Mostly Fourth Grade

Approach to Life. Age nine is, by and large, a year of equilibrium and a general calm similar to last year. She may begin quiet changes physically this year but the boys will usually not show significant outer development until next year. On the inside, however, she is working hard to form her own personality as a foundation for the upcoming stride toward the independence of adolescence. She is not fully aware of what she is doing, but much of the natural development is pulling her in a preparatory direction. Her desire to be with peers increases but she continues to need her parents, too. Age nine is a more mature version of age eight overall.

Identity. She wants her own identity and thus puts her personal stamp on everything she does. She has her own unique laughs, gestures, postures, and ways of explaining things. Nine will request increased independence *but probably will not show you the corresponding responsibility* she insists she can. She will want to be treated more like an adult despite a reputation (to you) that proves she is still a child. Other times the more adult-like side of her will shine through. Let her be that young adult when possible. This year, she will frequently be led more by her own internal motivation than by what happens around her or by what her friends are doing. She will have little awareness of any inconsistencies regardless of how often you point them out to her. Do not work too hard at trying to convince her how she really acts. She will be more reflective and pensive than she was during the previous year. Nine likes what she likes and does not like what she does not like. Favorite videos may get viewed many times a week.

Physical Development. She still looks girlish in most cases although some girls begin to develop breasts even at nine. Almost all of the boys still look like boys. Whatever the sex, be certain to enjoy what will probably be the *last year of true innocence.* Motion and exercise will continue at a nonstop pace but the increases in coordination often take great leaps this year. Almost any sport or activity will be done with enthusiasm. Chores do not count.

Emotional Reaction. This is a year of general emotional caution. At home, she may go off pensively to ponder the meaning of life. Her world opens up in complexity including an awareness of crime and a knowledge of disease and catastrophe. As result, more worries are common as is more compassion for the less fortunate.

Home Life. Family is important to Nine. She likes family activities though not always when the activities are offered. Free time is tremendously important. She probably needs reminders to take showers and brush her teeth daily for one more year. She may need reminders to put her dirty laundry in the hamper for the rest of her life.

Parents. Getting along with you should be relatively smooth this year. She appreciates praise though she will seldom seek it directly. Communication will improve a lot this year especially in her ability to paraphrase what you say and in giving feedback for your ideas and requests. Allow your nine-year-old to make more decisions that are appropriate for her age. Often, we parents get caught in a bind between making decisions for our children and blaming them for making inappropriate choices. They cannot learn to form effective conclusions without getting age-appropriate practice in making decisions. At the same time, try not offer more responsibility than she can actually handle. Even if she insists, raise your expectations of what she can do slowly.

Siblings. To be blunt, there is not much change in the next twelve months.

Peers. Being an individual is the major identity issue for the year in general. However, when it comes to her peers, *just belonging* is the standard. Conformity is strong and will get stronger. Both girls and boys form same-sex groups. Boys tend to create secret codes with special handshakes and group signals. Usually, any boy can join in especially if he has athletic prowess. The girls tend to form cliques although the memberships are usually still flexible. A strong moral sense of fairness and absolute "right and wrong" becomes solidified in their talk and beliefs, but this ethic often *does not* get carried over into peer interaction. The new morality toward others seldom, if ever, gets passed onto how she treats her siblings.

School. Often there is a major rise in expectations by teachers of fourth graders in terms of working independently both alone and in groups, organizing time and materials, and using self-discipline. Fortunately, Nine tends to make large gains in her attention span and ability to ignore distraction. These improvements are seen mostly at school. Your help and structure with homework will remain necessary for the vast majority.

Other Development. This is a good year to start specialty interests such as art, music, drama, gymnastics, computer, and magic. These activities will require your guidance but do not force drudgery. Children are good at *promising* to practice daily. Of course that was what they said about taking care of the puppy and feeding the kitten. Beware of forcing perfection or rigid schedules. Let their interests bring success and enjoyment too. Allow her to take ten lessons (a realistic agreement for this age) and then change to another specialty if she wants one. Be flexible, not overbearing. Begin another page in your About Me Book for extra-curricular developmental experts if you get into regular battles. Regarding my son's piano lessons, I had lunch with the music teacher at the school where I am the counselor to gain some hints on what to expect and what to enforce.

Age 10: Mostly Fifth Grade

Approach To Life. Year ten is typically the last year of being a kid and a year of general contentment. Greater reliability, a sense of having *good* luck, and a sincere striving to be fair are common at ten. And, oh, can he talk, talk, talk, to anyone who will listen. Preadolescence, with its personal upheaval and storms against authority are coming soon. If only ten could last forever for both parent and child.

Identity. He feels that most of life goes his way. Mr. Ten likes to complete tasks though not necessarily with elaboration. He feels he's just the right age to be: neither too old nor too young. He has sincere compassion for needy people and sick or endangered animals. Ten-year-olds are comfortable at home, school, and also when alone. Remember, of course, not all ten-year-olds will be exactly this way *much less for all twelve months of the year.*

Physical Development. Ten feels healthy. Girls often show early signs of puberty though few menstruate yet. Boys are generally behind in sexual awareness and do not ask many or sophisticated questions about either reproduction or romance for now. Girls' bodies often begin to show a less childish shape and boys gain more heft in the chest, shoulders, and legs this year.

Emotional Reactions. There is little complaining or worrying in year ten. Anger exists but is displayed in quick flares. His rage is frequently gone before you figure out what set him off. The humor tends to be slapstick. His focus is usually in the here and now. He loves to learn new facts and skills though not necessarily at the same time you are offering the lesson.

Home Life. Supper is easier now since Ten will try almost anything you serve. He is usually cooperative, although actually getting chores done still requires some supervision. When anger arises, he will stomp off muttering something about not being understood or never getting a fair chance. Remember that Ten calms quickly without much help, so allow him some peace on his own to quiet himself down. In general, he desires to please others and he is a devoted family member. He will rejoin the family soon and seldom pout alone extensively. Sadly, this will all ebb away, albeit *temporarily*, starting the next year for most children.

Parents. Girls want to go shopping mostly with Mom while boys increasingly chose to shop with Dad up to half the time when they have to go shopping. For the boys, looking for toys, video games, and sports or hobby equipment does not count as "shopping." Ten wants to be allowed to stay home alone for a few hours especially while his parents run errands instead of being dragged along. Simultaneously, he still looks forward to those bedtime chats, backrubs, and tuck-ins. Maybe *best of all, especially for Mom,* this is a year of appreciation for everything (okay, almost everything) that you do for him.

Siblings. Remember the anger that Ten has is intense but in short bursts? Since you are on the positive parent list for the year, guess who the primary targets of temper are? Remember also that the siblings, *especially the sweet darling types, are seldom as innocent* as they appear. Relationships with Ten's older siblings are commonly smooth, particularly if there are a few years in age between them.

Peers. Oh, how they love their friends! "Best friends forever" is often heard. Fairness is a paramount piece of loyalty. The boys tell dirty jokes, but do not ask them to explain the punchlines with any depth of understanding. Ten *does not* accept teasing or insults well this year although there are fewer tears when he feels wronged. He loves competition but is self-conscious in public if you pile on the acclaim.

School Life. He enjoys school in general although the academics are now viewed partly as a tolerable obstruction to chatting and playing with friends. Biographies and geography are popular topics. His teacher's approval is still important but this adult is no longer the centerpiece of his school day. Ten enjoys memorizing, rhyming, and building vocabulary through synonyms and antonyms. His writing reveals far greater detail and plot complexity than before.

Other Development. Morality and ethics are more absolute now and less flexible, although he often will not practice what he preaches *especially in competition.* Simultaneously, Ten begins to accept "white lies" as appropriate when used to protect someone else's feelings. Very little stealing and cheating are seen this year. He may curse to friends but his parents should never utter such things. In the very near future, you will not be able to help yourself!

Preparing For Preadolescence

Shirley is eleven years old going on twenty-five. She is an outgoing girl whose main complaints are that getting braces will ruin her life and that she does not have her own phone. She *was* a responsible student in the past. She tells her friends that her parents are total dimwits. Shirley is near the end of sixth grade, her first year of middle school.

Shirley's parents handle her very well. They usually listen to her point of view even when they disagree with her *illogical preteen logic.* They offer positive and negative consequences as fairly as possible while making fewer autocratic decisions. A mere year ago, there was far more mutual respect with Shirley. Now she insists that only her friends understand her. Shirley understands that, biologically, her parents were pre-grown-ups at one time, but wonders what mutations took place in their brains since then.

The past ended toward the end of fifth grade. Now the door to her room seems chronically closed. Her parents are not sure what she does in there but the portable phone is often in there with her and the music (?) is awfully loud. Shirley says her teachers are boring. She is her parents' oldest child — had her parents known that the preadolescent years were going to be like this, Shirley might have been an only child!

Unfortunately, many parents of preteen Shirleys perpetuate the *myth* of the ages eleven and twelve (starting as early as ten with some children and lasting well into year thirteen with others) as being battle-ridden for all in the household. The above description is common for part of this time, but it certainly is not complete. If your Shirley *was basically pleasant and respectful prior to turning eleven,* she will basically continue that way. Preadolescence is a time of identity shifting — from being a child to heading toward adulthood. Just as there was no handbook that accompanied Shirley's birth, there is no guidebook to tell her — and her parents — how to smoothly switch into the teenage years.

As the Shirleys change, so do we parents. The change will be rocky at times. But remember that those roller coasters of turbulence contain some wonderful surprise turns, too. To add to the challenge, no two preteens are alike. Further, you will not handle all your budding adults the same. And if you do find that age eleven is more tumultuous than it is positively exciting, here is a reminder that things get smoother for the vast majority at age twelve.

Some parents of preteens will tell me, "I was responsible when I was her age. I did my homework, I did chores when I was told, I enjoyed family outings." My typical response is, "Ask your parents what you were like between ages eleven and thirteen. I'll bet they have a different recollection." I asked my parents the same question about me a number of years ago. They asked me if I really wanted to hear the truth... I guess that explains my parents' unsympathetic snickering when I tell them about problems with my own preteens. My mother once commented, "So, how is the parenting expert faring this week?"

The preteen years are characterized by children suddenly claiming to have *all the answers* for handling their lives. This is often in direct opposition to our parental point of view that they have a lot to learn and need to realize the consequences of impulsive, or at least not fully informed, decisions. *Resist your impulse* to give lectures and snide comments.

Up to the preteen years, you have been teaching your children to "think for themselves" as a basis making sound decisions. You have also been encouraging them to be assertive about their views and values. A major parenting goal has been to provide a foundation for healthy independence. All these skills come to a head simultaneously amid this change in identity. Thus, it should not really be a surprise that significant emotional disruptions (your child's) and consequent family chaos emerges. Be sure to frequently review the earlier chapters "Emergencies and Buttons," "And It's Normal," and, of course, "Breathing to Ten."

Looking at this earliest part of adolescence, I have a list of "don't knows" that the average preteen is confused about. From moment to moment, Shirley *does not know:*

1. what she wants;

2. who she is now — although she did in the past;

3. how much she drives her parents crazy;

4. what mood is coming the next minute;

5. whether she wants her parents to be peers or protectors at any given time;

6. whether she wants parental guidance or to be left alone;

7. If she wants to be a child or a teen.

About all she is certain of is that she cannot get enough time with her friends. Additionally, she is quite certain that you parents seldom have as much spending money for her as she would like to have you give.

As her parents, you often will not know whether to feel sorry for Shirley or to send her to Antarctica for a year (since the odds are strong that next year will be much smoother for everyone). You will feel amazed that her energy is unending yet simultaneously feel a tinge depressed that you actually had that same level of energy yourselves once upon a time.

Shirleys everywhere will complain about *being treated like a child*. Although they are still children for the most part, they do not see that in themselves now. I explain to the Shirleys that I view freedom as the right to make choices, including *acceptance of both the positive and negative results* of those choices, but *not a right to do whatever they want* whenever they want to. Most of them understand this concept when calm and we parents are not acting authoritatively.

Then I explain to the parents of Shirleys that mutual respect and communication *with feedback* is vital this year. Teens and preteens need their parents as sounding boards to bounce ideas and responsibilities against.

I heard that a group of parents of Shirleys somewhere began a local support meeting called Parents of Ambivalent and Indecisive *Normal* Preteens (affectionally called PAIN). I hear the attendance is high... And during school lunches daily, everywhere, all the Shirleys are holding similar chat groups regarding how tough it is to live with parents these days.

Age 11: Mostly Sixth Grade

Approach to Life. She is Ms. Either-Or. Very little of life this year includes middle ground on opinions, feelings, and energy. She has decided that she does not want to be a child, *much less be treated like one,* anymore. Shedding her old identity and childhood role will not be smooth. This will be a tremendously serious year for everyone. It is a developmental period similar to toddlerhood. Once again, she says "no" to you frequently and does not really know what she wants — but she can certainly tell you what she does *not* want. And, like a wobbly toddler, she will not start preadolescence with clear direction or aplomb. Remember — *she has never done this preteen thing before.* Be firm but be compassionate, too. If she is your oldest child, neither have you. Middle school has a lot to do with this attitude shift. Or maybe this developmental shift was the reason for creating middle schools. Probably some of both.

Remember, too, the parenting joys of toddlerhood. Your daughter learned to explore, investigate, and challenge herself and her parents. For me, the terrible twos (as a parent, that is) were not very terrible as long as I remembered to *pick my battles carefully* and childproof the house thoroughly. At age eleven, we parents attempt to *world-proof* by protecting her from harm, negative influences, dangerous predicaments, and her own poor judgment when it surfaces. At the same time, her good judgment astounds us at times.

Your parental role is very important and necessary but do not expect her to give you credit just yet. Most of all, remember that if your Ms. Either-Or was happy, cooperative, and caring in the past, *she will return to be that same person* when she has had a year or so to gain some personal insights. Think of her best assets as merely going into temporary remission. Some of her best strengths will likewise jump out when you least expect them to. This is truly an up and down year. Eleven is a time for major change, but not war, although it my feel that way some days. Boys tend to be more defiant and directly confrontational. Girls tend to be more avoiding and ignoring. When in doubt, *offer her options and give her some time to choose.*

Identity. Eleven sees adults, of which you parents are her main representatives, as responsible for all her problems. However, you do not get the corresponding credit for her successes. Her sense of responsibility for her predicaments is at an all-time, but temporary, low. Try to *explain, not blame,* when discussing problems as best you can and as best as she will let you finish your illustration before becoming defensive. She gets defensive easily. You will get frustrated with this instant defensiveness. Much like spring cleaning, she has to *empty all of her identity shelves* before she can reorganize them. This is a year of pulling everything down. This is the year of anti-identity.

Physical Development. "Can't you just sit still for a moment!" is a familiar parental phrase. The answer is "no!" whether she says it aloud or not. The biological energy of puberty is either starting to boil or is gurgling just beneath the surface. She is like Yellowstone's Old Faithful geyser: either building up steam or going off. Silly gestures and slapstick foolery are chronic this year. She will eat voraciously, although she is finicky again. Much like most of year eleven, she adores a certain food or despises it. At least for this week, that is. Do not waste your energy arguing with this fickleness: peanut butter and jelly sandwiches were probably created by the parent of an eleven-year-old.

Boys start puberty anywhere between ten and fifteen, although eleven through thirteen are the most common inauguration years. Erections are frequent results of almost any type of stimulation. Masturbation becomes regular mostly as a release of the pressure that accompanies the erection *more than from sexual ideation* or sensual fantasy. Scrotum growth, pubic hair, and penis enlargement usually come along about a year or more later.

Girls start puberty anywhere between nine and fifteen, with ages eleven and twelve being common commencement years. Physical changes include widening at the hips, the appearance of pubic hair, first periods, breast development, and height spurts. Girls are usually a year ahead of the boys in general sexual development. Physical and emotional development *do not* necessarily occur simultaneously, which is certainly true when the physical changes appear at either the early or late ends of the nine-to-fifteen age range.

Emotional Reactions. Anger and love are the most regularly displayed emotions aimed at parents. Her confidence seems high and she consistently acts as though she knows all she needs to know to handle any situation. Or at least this is the attitude she displays on the surface. Do not let this bravado fool you. Internally, *she is often depending upon you to set limits.* There are many fears at eleven about nightmares, darkness, being left alone in an emergency, being hurt by bullies or gangs, and school grades and taking tests. Crying is frequent since there is so much confusion inside her head. Life is expressed in extremes with little middle-of-the-road energy or statements. Both ends of her emotional continuum are sincere, so refrain from embarrassing her during her times of neediness and insecurity. Do not remind her of her bids for independence and power from a few hours earlier. It is frequently difficult to tell when she is wanting you to leave her alone and when she wants you to act parentally restrictive. The difficulty is increased because she often does not know which role she wants you to play either.

Home Life. Don't get your hopes high for the grown-up part of her to clean up the house or even neaten her room.

Eleven's definition of independence often means "mess." She seems to dislike all organization including bedtime and rules — although she will readily admit that rules and chores are needed for everyone else. Eleven will often expend more energy avoiding or arguing about her chores than just doing them cooperatively. She has no idea how difficult she is to live with and you will wasting your breath trying to convince her of this (although *you* may feel better after delivering a twenty minute lecture). Surprisingly, since we have been discussing Eleven's seeming anti-family values, she *enjoys being involved* in family decisions, meals, and outings.

Parents. Your role is summed up in two phrases: (1) "I need you (according to my schedule)" and (2) I don't need you (at least not this instant)." Keep reaching out to her to do activities together. Despite her frequent rejections, try not to take her avoidances personally. However, *do respond to her surly manner and attitude* concerning respectfulness *but not with punishment* often. If you do punish repeatedly, Eleven will end up being grounded for the whole decade while you will also be kept home-bound enforcing the sentence! If, and when, you punish her, make the consequences short in duration and certainly not physical past age ten. (I am aware that many parents, and even some school personnel, encourage paddling recalcitrant children up to the start of high school. However, I believe strongly that corporal punishment after elementary school models the message that "might makes right" in direct opposition to the message of seeking effective and cooperative solutions we want our children to learn. See the section on punishment later in this book for further explanation of effective discipline for all middle childhood ages.) Adding a chore is best and doing it with her can work well... sometimes. Again, remember that her disappointing you is not her goal but rather a by-product of her need to *disagree with anyone not her age* or considered to be admirable in her mind. Applaud her efforts and successes often. She really is listening to your opinions but must follow "the code of elevens" which means she cannot let you know she is listening. How you respond to her behaviors will set the tone for how she treats her own preadolescents (your grandchildren) in the future.

Regarding Mom: the brunt of Eleven's emotional garbage is usually hurled at you. Dad won't observe many of these onslaughts of verbiage and character assassination, so he my think you are being overly sensitive. Not so!

Regarding Dad: Eleven, the female version, is turning into a woman and can stir sexual feelings inside you. Do not shy away and *do not withhold your hugs.* She still needs her dad's parental physical affection, but do be more careful where you touch her. Discuss any emotional discomforts you experience with your wife, trusted friends, and colleagues of both sexes. See your consult list and keep adding to it. If sexual abuse existed in your childhood talk to a counselor. Refer to the chapter on Getting Help.

Siblings. Did I say Mom gets the majority of Eleven's free-flowing verbal venom? Well, her younger siblings get massive doses, too, especially if they are close in age. Of course, the younger sibs start some of these battles as well. Set guidelines as to how the siblings are to solve their disagreements or send them both off to calm down. Review the Normals Family chapters if you need reminders on dealing with sibling troubles. Also see Problem Solving activities in the final section of this book and peruse the bibliography.

Siblings who are much older than Eleven are seldom targets. In fact these older brothers and sisters can often be helpful mediators and counselors for Eleven after a stormy encounter with you.

Peers. Friendships continue as the paramount focus of her energy. Boys seek boys and girls seek girls most often, although some girls will acknowledge that boys may have

some favorable attributes. The peer group code strictly includes *not tattling* to adults, although Eleven usually understands that serious problems such as drugs, alcohol, or suicidal comments are to be reported to parents or teachers. Supervised activities, teams, extra-curricular classes, scouts, and so forth, are beneficial to building social skills and burning off social energy. If she cannot choose an activity, offer some options. Be careful not to force the choice *you* want for her.

She loves sleep-overs but be certain to set a *few* top-priority rules *firmly*. Sleep lightly and investigate loud arguments, especially ones that involve the exclusion of certain guests. Check up on strange noises. Also beware of long periods of silence.

School Life. Middle school can be overwhelming. There is no longer a central teacher to watch over her. She may have crushes on favorite opposite-sex teachers. Other than lunch, passing notes and gossip are often the highlights of the school day.

Eleven continues to need supervision and help with homework. You will need help to help her with some assignments and in planning how to complete long-term projects since the information and independence of the work gets quite complex in sixth grade. Let her choose a time and place to study so long as she does it when she says she will and the quality of work is up to yours and the teachers' standards. *Check her work* even she insists it is complete and error-free.

Other Development. Give love regularly even if she spurns your affections this year. Never, never, initiate displays of affection in public or in front of friends. Of course, she can initiate hugs and kisses anytime. If there is a history of her avoiding you or repeatedly pulling away from your affections, see the Getting Help chapter as this is a symptom of deeper family problems.

Eleven has a new passion: the bargain. She loves to offer deals such as, "You do the dishes tonight, Dad, and I'll vacuum the house Saturday morning." Usually she sincerely intends to keep her half of the agreement *when the deal is made.* Be alert that Saturday's promised chore will frequently be troublesome and fraught with excuses. When the next deal is offered, just be sure *she does her part first* to wipe the deal-slate clean. Then start the deal process again with a spirit of "innocent until guilty." This is a healthy cycle.

Do not expect her to fully comprehend the cause-and-effect relationships such as the fact that she cannot go outside until the vacuuming is completed. Eleven has not yet totally developed this concept and she will, to some extent, sincerely feel victimized. If you are convinced she never had any intention of performing her part of the contract, again, have her do her part first next time. But do not hold a grudge.

Age 12: Mostly Seventh Grade

Approach to Life. Just when you were about to run away from home yourself, year twelve hits like a Caribbean breeze. Okay, that is a bit of an exaggeration, but for some families, the change in seventh grade is a dramatically positive and welcome change. Your son seems calmer, less cantankerous, more cooperative — more at ease with himself and his life. He even gives you respect as if he were ten years old again. Anger and impulsivity show more restraint. Twelve has a greater sense of how others feel as well as of his effect upon others. Much like when he was in first grade, life feels pretty good. The crazy, all-is-new life of the previous years' introduction to middle school is under much better control. *Composure is back.*

Identity. Twelve is less anti-adult and more pro-grown-up in his general attitude. He can observe himself more objectively regarding his strengths and weaknesses, but he still needs your guidance to avoid over focusing on his deficits when stressed. Encourage him to *change the failings that are changeable* and *accept the failings he cannot alter.* He cannot change his height but he can improve his posture. He cannot correct his lack of coordination but he can practice both sports and artwork. Equally important, help him accept that we are all a mixture of assets and deficits. Most of the negative aspects we see in ourselves are of little concern to our friends. Look back at your own buttons if you find yourself overreacting to your child's shortcomings in comparison to your helping him focus on his areas of pride.

Physical Development. The energy of year eleven is still apparent, but is more focused on goals and more under his control. The athletes and the non-athletes of both sexes separate more openly for sports, with the more competitive, powerful, and agile players usually staying on formal teams. Changes in sexual development are obvious this year although many twelves are still in the early or beginning stages. For a few, usually girls, puberty can be in full bloom. A number of the boys' voices start to get lower, pubic hair may start to appear, and penis size may be increasing a bit. Masturbation, which has existed since toddlerhood, now includes larger erections and ejaculation. As parents, explain the naturalness of masturbation, especially since most twelve year-old boys are just starting to see the reproduction process as *more than dirty pictures* and nudity. Help him to understand both sexuality and sensuality. Playing with his penis is primarily physical enjoyment at this time. For most boys, the greatest physical and sexual growth spurts occur between ages 13 and 15.

For the girls, this is commonly a year of major changes. Top height may have already been reached. Breasts gain a rounder, more mature, shape but usually are not of full size yet. Year twelve is the most common year for a first period. Be sure she understands the menstruation process so she is not scared or surprised, and does not feel unhealthy — emotionally or sexually — about the physical start of womanhood. The same is true for her masturbating since girls are more secretive about this although clitoral and vaginal stimulation is common. Do not depend upon the school's sex education programs to do all the explaining. Your manner of educating sets the tone for how she will see herself as a sexual adult. The same for boys, too.

Emotional Reactions. Enthusiasm for friends, activities, and goals is very high. Fortunately, there is less and less enthusiasm for arguing with you for the mere sake of arguing. Insults of the pain-intentioned variety are less frequent although they still do pop up. Twelve still has fears — of punishments, getting in trouble at home and school, and social worries of losing friends and being avoided by peers for any number of reasons from body odor to pimples.

Continuing fears from the past include being in the dark, being kidnapped, being left alone unexpectedly, and getting lost. Masturbation by both sexes (including teens and adults) commonly increases when stress is present to serve as a temporary distraction, comfort, and/or tension reducer. High cholesterol is clearly not a major concern for him yet, which most fast food restaurants are happy to know.

Home Life. Twelve's general reasonableness improves toward everyone. He is more helpful, more aware of living with others. Self-entertainment is up and dependence upon TV is down. He is even less fussy about what is served for supper as well as who sits next to him during the meal.

Parents. Twelve is more tolerant of his parents' views. This does not mean he agrees with you, but rather that he is more willing to hear your opinions. He is more accepting of you having your own lives and your needs to be alone without children present. Twelve sees you as fairer in your decisions. All in all, he is much nicer to be around.

Siblings. He is more accepting of those same sibs he considered "such little brats" in the recent past. Of course (pun intended), this is a relative tolerance. Twelve is more helpful with much younger siblings. Older sibs, especially if in college or late high school, may be placed on pedestals. And, since Twelve is friendlier, those so-called brats are usually acting less bratty in response... that is, unless *they* are now ten years old.

Peers. Not counting use of the phone, Twelve can be summed up by the two-m's: movies and malls. Make that *3-m's: money* for the movies and malls. Interest in the opposite sex increases but remains mostly latent this year especially for boys. Break-ups of friendships are less volatile now and more platonic in tone. Co-ed parties may start but same-sex sleep-overs are still top fun. Teasing is present though less acerbic. He will profit by continued participation in structured extra curricular activities.

School. If your twelve year-old is still harboring anger in massive doses, school is the most likely target. The love, or at least the desire, to learn wanes until high school, although a peppy, challenging, and joking-but-structured teacher is still appreciated. On school mornings, he can get himself out of bed and ready to leave with 90 percent reliability.

Other Development. Drug and alcohol use and experimentation are unlikely at age twelve but can occur. Sadly, first uses occur at younger and younger ages today. If you suspect usage, get an assessment at a mental health or chemical dependency evaluation center. Do not take a chance. At young ages, *addiction takes hold far faster than with adults.*

Although ethics and moral behavior continue to be held in high importance, cheating is more accepted as understandable under certain circumstances as opposed to being viewed as the character flaw it was deemed a few years earlier. As parents, we need to keep the pressure on for responsible behavior. Of course, we need to model what we preach.

Middle childhood is over now for most children, although some of the late bloomers may just be starting preadolescence. Further, many children do not develop in the same area at the same time. Numerous boys and girls develop socially ahead or behind their physical changes. Do not try to rush or slow any of these growth areas. Do set limits on their freedom and choices as necessary. Remember that preadolescents are very aware of themselves in comparison to their contemporaries: be sensitive to their sensitivity.

End Of Childhood - Age 13 to the End Of High School

This stage is the end of basic childrearing for parent and child alike. Both of you struggle between letting go and holding on. There is simultaneous excitement and worry for the future felt by both teen and parent. And just when you or your teen thinks he has a handle on things, one or the other of you shifts. Recall how development for adults is seldom stagnant. The battles and affections run strong because the stakes for both are high regarding the future and your feeling that you have to get your idea across now-or-never. Sexual issues bring up many buttons for parents — fears, ethics, religion — as well as a chance to rethink one's own adolescence. The fact is that about one-half of teens try some form of sex before the end of high school. In addition, dating usually begins sometime after the start of ninth grade. The peer pressure for the teen is tremendous. Peer pressure is the influence of one's same-age group. The more well-adjusted her friends are, *the more positive their influence* on her. The more irresponsible her friends are, the less accountable she will be. Refrain from seeing all teens as the same. They certainly are *not*. The social pressure to have one's child appear successful in the parent's peer circle is also tremendous. By and large, teens encounter temptations with vast consequences matched with increasingly skilled judgement. Their main consultants now are their friends — whose judgment is also improving. The older our children get, the more willing they are to consider our opinions. If their safety is at risk, take a firmer hand while they are still at home. Otherwise, slowly let go as best you can.

As parents, *listen to your teen.* Understand her perspective and avoid forcing unsolicited advice upon her. As your teen nears adulthood, her abilities to observe the world and herself, to consider options, to use insight and reasoning, and to reach sensible conclusions grows remarkably. Strive to keep your comments short without moralizing. Adolescents continue to need your guidance, however, your underlying tone must say, "I trust and respect you." Avoid demanding obedience as this injures your relationship (at any stage) and is less and less possible to enforce after age sixteen anyway. The messages at this stage are:

1. "I will help you figure out who you are as you approach young adulthood." Your parental role is now more that of a counselor than a task-master. Knock on her bedroom door and hold short chats. When you force your way in, all you do is invade her privacy and encourage her to secure her boundaries even more. Goals and viewpoints can still shift between the pragmatic and the idealistic since your child comprehends both positions, especially at the older end of the stage. To help with idealism, encourage your teen to be involved with community service via school projects, church programs, hospital

volunteering, and so forth.

2. "I will help you discover where affection, sensuality, and sexual activity merge. I admit that these issues may be particularly tough for me since they were not given very clearly to me." Most parents grew up with less openness concerning the discussion of sexuality. Many of us parents had the *one big lesson* on human reproduction with a few follow-up lessonettes. Sex is just an aspect of life and is best handled on an ongoing basis. Television, movies, and the news will give you endless opportunities to add information, give opinions, and ask questions. You do not have to be an expert to discuss sex or any other topic. Your child may have the vocabulary for covering sexuality but not necessarily have a grasp of the concepts to accompany it.

3. "I encourage you to develop your own interests and relationships." When you feel your child has made poor decisions, give her either-or options so that those poorer choices are less available. *Do not make decisions for her that she can make for herself,* as she will not learn to make sensible ones without practicing.

4. "You can be *independent* — by yourself or with friends — and also be dependent — a part of this family." Allow for her dual membership and identity.

5. "I will continue to support and protect you as much as I can when you need me." This includes restricting harmful relationships (abusive dates, peer drug users), getting drug treatment if abuse is suspected, seeking police protection if your

daughter is threatened or hurt repeatedly. She still needs her parents to intercede when problems get out of her control such as continually failing grades or when she requires medical treatment. If you do not rescue her from such actual emergencies, then you abdicate your parental responsibility. She is counting on you to be her life-guard in a crisis although she may seldom admit it. However, be sure to try to *solve these problems with her instead of for her* whenever possible .

6. "I enjoy both the child parts and the adult parts of you although I do not always know which one I am talking to." This is the unconditional love message. It states that humor and acceptance go together. You are promising to try to laugh at life's foibles with her, to laugh at yourself, and to make a commitment *not to laugh at her.* Sometimes you can discern a humorous perspective from perceived insult by mutually telling each other that your feelings were hurt by a comment and explaining why the remark was offensive to you. As explained in the earlier section on humor, accept that your statement or joke upset her regardless of your intent. You do not have to agree with her reaction. You do, however, have to *treat her feelings with respect.* Do not be surprised if a comment you made was taken with offense one day and repeated to her friend with laughter a few days later. If she makes your previously injurious remark into a joke directly to you, question her about her turnabout of views. She may have valid reasons and she may not be aware of her inconsistency. Use these situations as teachable moments.

*****

As a college admissions officer once said of teenage independence, "The bad news is you will frequently not know what she is actually doing since she will be off on her own... *The good news* is that you usually will not know what she is actually doing since she will be off on her own..." Trust her, respect her, and be there to support her when she needs you.

SECTION 6.

INTRODUCTION TO DISCIPLINE & INTERVENTIONS

By the time you have reached this section, your sense of peace, as cited in this book's subtitle, has probably improved already. You looked at your parenting style, considered your emotional panic buttons, and assessed your handling of anger, guilt, and grief. You have learned when a parent-child problem is basically normal and when to get professional help. You now have a greater understanding of what behavior is appropriate for your child's developmental age. You have more confidence in yourself as a parent and in your teamwork with your spouse. But something may still be amiss. Ten-year-old Armanda's fury at her younger sister still has you spending half of your free time breaking up the battles between them. Tim, age seven, throws tantrums every time you tell him to clean his room. Kathy, turning twelve this week, bitterly insists she is old enough to go on dates and has kept up this demand for freedom for over a month.

The title also refers to gaining greater cooperation from your children during these middle childhood years. Attaining this cooperation takes self-discipline by both you (as the model) and your child, as well as parental discipline whereby you motivate and provide consequences.

There are a number of *goals of discipline:*

1. to increase your child's ability to solve problems for his age;

2. to help him explore and experiment in his world

carefully (we want to encourage curiosity together with a sense of caution);

3. to build his tolerance for frustration;

4. to enable him to see himself with humility — but to neither humiliate others nor tolerate others humiliating him);

5. to learn how to avoid repeating mistakes while increasing his successes in life.

Our responsibilities *as parents* are:

1. to love, protect, and shelter our children;

2. to teach them how to get along with others;

3. to provide them with opportunities, challenges, and responsibilities they can handle according to their ages and abilities;

4. to help them build esteem based upon both their efforts and their results.

Children require innumerable opportunities for trial and error in learning about their world. They must experiment to be certain that what seemed to be the cause of trouble really was the factor at fault. In an equally scientific vein, successes need to be replicated to identify the specific factors that will enhance repeated triumphs in the future. These tasks are not easy for us or for our children. However, the journey of helping our children develop into young adults is mostly a satisfying and enjoyable trip.

Parental discipline will certainly include punishments such as loss of privileges, groundings, lowering curfews, adding extra chores, and setting behavior limits appropriate for the infraction. *I do not encourage spanking* in middle childhood and strongly discourage its use after age nine. A swat or two at younger ages can be effective when your child blatantly refuses to stop a behavior or defiantly opposes a repeated command although, even then, spanking should be done sparingly. Spanking is an expression of a power battle that almost always begets future battles. When used in middle childhood struggles for power may get the winner a *short-term* victory. Yet, in the long run, trust, cooperation, and motivation are hindered. Whenever possible, parental discipline should be a positive teaching tool using reasoning, incentives, and compromise. Again, there will be times — more times with some children than with others — that punishments will be necessary. If punishment is common in your home try a new tack. If your new approach does not result in immediate positive results, remain patient. Try again. Do not quit your new methods too quickly. At times, we parents need to be scientists, too. However, when a new approach is not effective either, seek help.

The most effective discipline methods encourage mutual respect between parent and child (at least in the long run), are based on arranging child safety, build a sense of fairness, and take the individual child into consideration. Your oldest child may be more responsible in general and is often referred to as "mature" by other parents. Discipline may seldom be necessary for him. His younger brother may be less receptive to adult-types of reasoning and may require more material and more immediate incentives than his older brother did to gain compliance with household rules. Be careful in offering ongoing rewards to the younger sibling as this punishes the older child because *he did do what you asked.* Short-term rewards, however, may be helpful when used judiciously. As with Cindy and Mindy Normal's arguments, offering joint rewards can be significantly effective since it encourages the siblings to remind each other to cooperate with your parental guidelines and rules. Again, use this incentive system judiciously or its effectiveness becomes stale. Further, refer to the appropriate developmental section of this book to determine your child's level of maturity. A young child goes after what he wants with little regard to potential dangers: the knife looks shiny, the plug fits neatly into the socket. As parents, we redirect the youngster to his colored blocks, removing the knife or placing socket protectors in the outlets. By middle childhood, we hope that such preschool-age behavior is long behind. Remember that children who are overly anxious or have ADHD tend to be less mature in handling problems. Treat each child according to his emotional and social age when there is stress or stubbornness instead of by his actual chronological age.

Last, as parent teams in two-parent families and or as divorced parents, *you do not have to agree* on how to handle your children. The schools, the neighborhood, and the home usually have differing expectations, incentives, and disciplinary techniques from one another as well. The most important concern is that all parents — married parents, single parents, stepparents, even grandparents — are *consistent but not rigid* in their *individual* styles. Your consistency allows the child to predict the positive and negative consequences he is most likely to receive from you. Although parents do not always need to be in agreement about behavioral goals and permissions for the same child, *each parent involved with a particular child does need to back the other* parent's decisions *in front of that child* — otherwise the child is encouraged to be both negatively manipulative to get what he wants as well as to have various parents engage in power battles between them so that the child escapes responsibility for his own behavior. Both adults need to be able to at least consider the validity in criticisms made by the other. In addition, each parent needs to encourage the child to respect the other parent in order to prevent placing the child in a position of having to choose one parent as the "best" in comparison to the other. Certainly, this is easier said than done, *especially in divorced families.* When you find that you and your spouse disagree in depth and seemingly cannot compromise, use the problem-solving approach described in this section: again, the scientific approach is recommended. Try a new solution to your child's problem for a limited time and keep track of the results. Be certain to re-read the first section of this book to see where the inflexibilities you both experience are really coming from.

As you read through this section on interventions and discipline, you will probably find yourself feeling more comfortable with some techniques than with others. Equally, you will probably sense that some activities will be more effective with one of your children than with one of his siblings. Mix and match interventions as needed in the laboratory of parenthood.

The ability to listen to one another is a basic communication skill we perform daily. Yet, all of us encounter situations in which we find that listening to someone else is difficult to do. At these uncomfortable times, we need to know the specific components of this communication act in order to make the necessary modifications for success.

Effective Listening - Part I

Listening is a one-on-one boundary exercise. It is a healthy boundary exercise because it lets your child (or spouse) take responsibility for solving his own problem at his own pace. In other words, you get to help the other person help himself. You do not need to worry about providing the right advice because advice is seldom needed here. The focus is on the individual child, not on family goals.

In situations in which effective listening is used, the problem or concern — such as low grades, arguments with friends, or other individual predicaments — belongs to one person. You, the parent, are the counselor and consultant. The problem does not directly affect you, although you can certainly feel sympathy or experience strong emotions depending upon your personal reaction to his dilemma.

The boundary surrounds the responsibility for the problem and how it should be solved. If the problem belongs primarily to your child, then it does *not* belong to you. A family room couch belongs to all living in the house and its care would be listed under family concerns. For now, however, we are talking about individual issues. When your child solves his own problems, *he gets the credit* and his self-respect rises as a result. It is important to put your views aside: help him put his situation into terms he can use to frame his problem and its possible solutions. Instead of possibly ignoring you or arguing with you about your ideas, he will appreciate you for your attention *and your trust* in letting him handle his own predicament. The long-term effect is that he will feel freer to talk to you about the big stuff when he is older and the stakes of misjudgment are higher.

The components of effective listening include helping your child to describe his situation clearly. *When we are upset, all the parts of our dilemma tend to run together in such a way that no one piece can be isolated for repair.* The listener's first role is to identify the feelings discussed in order to help the speaker identify the emotions at hand. Feelings are mixed up in the jumble and are in need of isolation also. The next parental task is to guide the child toward finding his own solutions, easing the feelings of panic and helplessness that we all experience when pressured and stressed.

As an example, an eleven-year-old girl named Jennifer tells her mother that something is bothering her. Jenny feels like dropping out of the soccer team despite the season being half over. This would be the second year in a row she has quit a team, as well as recently quitting the school yearbook committee. Her mother patiently asks Jenny to explain the dilemma and what Jenny feels her options are. As Jenny talks — she is actually thinking aloud in Mom's presence — Mom periodically summarizes for Jenny by rephrasing what she says. Let's continue.

Jenny: "The other girls don't like me, the coach doesn't let me play much, and those stupid team uniforms are scratchy."

Mom: "Hmm. It sounds like you do not think anyone else respects you or wants you playing on their team." Mom thinks to herself, "I hope Jenny does not quit another activity — no wonder her coach and teammates do not take her seriously."

Jenny: "And they tease me for not being any good and for not trying hard enough. They tease me for quitting all the time." She pauses for a moment. "I guess I could practice a bit at home between games but I don't like getting all sweaty. The uniforms itch even more when I sweat."

Mom: "Sounds like you feel as if you lose no matter what you do."

Jenny: "I guess I'll have to finish the season this time. Maybe you and Dad can practice with me sometimes, okay? Well, I gotta go call Suzie about the big science test tomorrow."

Mom: "Wait!" But Jenny is already in the next room, dialing. "What big science test? Yesterday you said there weren't any tests this week...Jenny!!!"

Mom admits to herself that Jenny has pretty good insight some days. Mom's not quite sure how Jenny reached that decision about practicing soccer more often based on what Jenny told her, but the conclusion sounded okay.

Jenny's mother did not force her own opinions on Jenny. By withholding her own solutions, Mom allowed Jenny to reach her own decision, which was probably the same conclusion Mom would have advised. And Mom earned Jenny's trust by respecting Jenny's boundaries through listening and reflecting. Mom was feeling *parent reputation* stress as other parents at the soccer games had been everheard snickering about whether Jenny would show up to the games or not. When our family image is mentioned, then keeping the boundaries straight becomes more clouded. Mom made the right choice here. Jenny's responsibility to her team was the primary issue.

As with all parenting techniques, *there are times when effective listening is neither appropriate nor effective.* For example, if Jenny cannot find her soccer cleats because her room is a mess, the missing cleats are Jenny's own problem. Effective listening be can helpful after she finds the shoes and attends practice. If missing cleats become a regular problem, then another approach is required such as the upcoming "forced choices" and "natural consequences." At age eleven, Jenny is capable of organizing her room so that she does not repeatedly lose her shoes. This organizing ability should exist assuming Jenny does not have ADHD or a learning disability: both of these conditions interfere with organizing, selecting practical solutions, and following through responsibly with those solutions. Note, *I did not say these learning conditions make organizing impossible for the child, just more difficult.*

However, if Jenny continually leaves the kitchen a mess after eating her afterschool snack, this is a family problem since the kitchen is a family area. Jenny's demolition of the kitchen affects the family, or at least the parents, who are most likely to notice the chaos of crumbs and wrappers. In the case of messes in community areas such as kitchens, family rooms, and hallways, see the upcoming interventions regarding "contracts," "forced choices," and "family roundtable discussions." (Some wives claim that some husbands can be like children in their tendency to ignore messes or that some men may suffer from a disability I call "selective blindness" to household havoc...At this time, I will choose to save my opinion on this volatile topic for another book that will be published no earlier than the year 2008.)

*****

Effective listening, with its accompanying respect for letting a person be responsible — according to his developmental age — for solving his own problems, is a sign of family health. This communication technique is a foundation for many of the interventions that follow. The next chapter provides further explanation and examples of listening skills. If calm listening is especially difficult for you to use with your children, then there are most probably underlying power battles going on. If effective listening is uncomfortable for you, *practice* with a friend, with your friend acting as if he or she is your child. If that is not helpful, seek help.

There are entire books written on listening skills (see bibliography). Since this skill is so basic for honest communication and for solving problems between people, an additional example is given. Remember, remember, remember: this activity has just a few guidelines and it is a relatively simple task. But if either participant is under stress, much less if there is mutual pressure felt, this is not an easy task by any means at all. At the close of this chapter, additional hints will be given on how to make effective listening become even more effective.

Effective Listening: Part 2

Mr. & Mrs. Aybeesee came to my office complaining that their nine-year-old son Luke was continually blaming his teacher for his misbehavior at school. According to the teacher, Luke was frequently rude to her although he interacted well with his peers. His parents re-enacted a chat they had with Luke a few days before .

Dad: "How were things with Mrs. Math today?"

Luke: "She's still being stupid about not letting us chew gum in class. She made me miss recess again. Blah, blah, blah (in a complaining, it's-not-my-fault tone)."

Dad (interrupting): "Quit your whining! Mrs. Math is the teacher. She makes the classroom rules. And you'd better do what she tells you or I'll give you something to really complain about!"

Luke (yelling): "You never listen to me! You always take the teacher's side!" Then Luke huffed off muttering something about how all grown-ups are the same.

I explained that although Luke certainly had a demanding tone and inappropriate attitude about setting his own rules at school, that Luke was right about his father's poor listening. "You do not listen to him. I am not saying at all that Luke should be rude to his teacher, but that is a separate issue from your not listening to his view of the problem. Let's take one part at a time. First, the listening. Remember that *mutual respect is based upon hearing the other person's viewpoint* and trying to understand it. *Whether or not you agree is not important in effective listening.* Healthy boundaries allow for your son to be responsible for his own issues. The message you gave Luke by interrupting and lecturing about teacher-as-boss was that he is not capable of finding an eventual solution. And, we may find, he is not capable of solving this problem without your intervention, but that is a separate issue to be tackled later.

I continued to explain about the effective listening aspect in the case of the Luke versus the Teacher. "When you ask Luke a question, let him answer it. In this instance, let him rant about Mrs. Math's unfairness for a few minutes. To help you keep your perspective, assume that Luke is telling the truth as he sees it. In almost every difference of opinion there is some truth and accuracy in both viewpoints. Then, remembering that this is mostly Luke's problem, not yours, *acknowledge his truth* as he sees it. Then ask him *what he can do to* help remedy the situation. Periodically summarize what he says to help him clarify his feelings and views. Effective listening is more than merely listening. It also involves re-phrasing his position and clarifying his ranting statements so he has a workable problem formed in his mind. Last, do not expect an immediate answer because he may have to ponder his problem and his options for awhile. If you are not adept at effective listening, try it with less volatile topics than disrespecting authority. Try topics such as favorite teams, preferable television shows, future hopes and goals, laws he would like to change, what he would do if her were president, and so on. *Give yourself credit for trying* this activity for at least the first twenty times you use it.

"Of course," I added. "If his rudeness with his teacher does not stop quite quickly after the effective listening, schedule a parent-teacher conference with Mrs. Math. Do not assume automatically that either Luke or his teacher is at fault. There may be academic or significant authority problems involved. It is better to set the meeting at school *too quickly* and happily find out the problem is already improving than to wait until the problem is out of hand before you contact the school."

*****

There are circumstances where effective listening is clearly the intervention of choice and situations in which it should only be used cautiously if at all. Effective listening is very helpful when used to intervene with depressed moods caused by the death of a relative, friend, or pet, divorce, following a house or school fire, or subsequent to any tragedy or incident your child perceives as a tragedy. Your listening to and reframing of his comments allows his feelings to become more organized in his mind. *Your attention provides support for his misery as a legitimate reason for sorrow.* If his talk is preponderantly about his loss, limit the listening you give him and then change the subject. *Resist* giving him banal advice such as "It will be better soon," or "You will get over it", or "Who ever said life would be easy," or "This will make you a stronger person in the future," and so on. Such comments trivialize the obvious non-triviality he experiences. Although he most probably will eventually cope with this intense issue, now is not the time to tell him. Review how well he coped with the grief at a later time.

In situations of ongoing over-anxiety, use effective listening sparingly *before* the dreaded event, test, trip, whatever. Although your young worrier hopes to find a panacea to guarantee a happy ending, ongoing talk prior to the event actually does the opposite: it increases his fears of the upcoming occasion. Do listen, just not at length. However, do not belittle his fears, as *they are real to him.* Explain that *over-focusing on the future raises dread* instead of reducing it. While you listen beforehand, assess whether there are any safety issues that *do require* your intervention and, as an appropriately protective parent, act accordingly. Later, after the occasion, use your listening skills at greater length. Have him discuss his emotions and explain how he survived or succeeded after the event is over.

Just as effective listening is the foundation skill for successful communication, the decision-making skills explained in this chapter are the basis for reaching practical solutions to problems that arise in life. You and your child can use the problem-solving skills for interpersonal, family, marital, work, financial, and personal problems. As in all effective interventions, keep your decisions as simple and as short-term as possible. Hint: step four is the most often skipped step. Don't skip it.

No Easy Decisions

Your ten-year-old daughter plans to do her homework before supper so she can watch a favorite television show at 7:30. At 6:30, she remembers that her best friend Gloria wanted to do science together at 7:00. She realizes that she cannot do both. She pouts for a moment and then, as you have modeled for her so many times, she follows the four step problem-solving process:

1. "I have this dilemma," she begins. She is admitting that there is a problem. This is a good first step. Peace and cooperation are on the way. She realizes that she cannot solve any problem as long as she denies that a quandary exists. Her attitude tells you that she believes a solution can be found, although following that solution may not be easy. She adds, "And there is something that can be done." She accepts that a solution can be found that will at least make her situation better than it is now. Depression is ruled out by her optimism.

2. "I have a number of options," she continues. She is aware that *there is more than one solution* that can work. These options can include asking her parents, siblings, friends, or teachers for help as she feels she needs assistance. She then lists the options for consideration: (a) have her brother tape the television show and keep the homework date with Gloria; (b) ignore the plans with her friend and apologize profusely in her best airhead, "oh-I-forgot" act if Gloria calls or asks her about it tomorrow at school; (c) ask Mom or Dad to call the Gloria's parents and say she just came down with pneumonia but that she'll be fine in time for school tomorrow; (d) miss the show this week and ask some friends what happened in tonight's episode.

She considers the strengths and weaknesses of each option, recognizing that every decision has both positive and negative aspects — that *there is no perfect decision.* She is already feeling more confident in her problem-solving skills. Although ten year-olds can actually work through this process independently, they will often ask for ideas or help. Help as best you can, but do not make her decision for her. Just lead her down the decision path. Encourage her to consider the solutions that may not look good at first. Most of those lesser options will look pretty weak later on, but it is good to add them to the list. A weak idea may be combined with a better plan to make it even better.

These first two steps are attitudinal. The following steps are behavioral. When a child is depressed, she stops either at step one due to hopelessness (she feels that there are no possible solutions) or at step two due to helplessness (she feels that there are workable solutions but that *she* is personally unable to find or perform one). Anxious children will stop at either of the behavioral steps below since they are good "talkers" but poor "doers" due to their fear of imperfection and low confidence to perform tasks adequately. A child who does step three but not step four is "quitting while she is ahead," a way of saying her success was due to luck instead of her personal skill.

3. Your daughter continues. "My plan is to ask my brother to tape the show and meet Gloria. I will watch it over the weekend. On the plus side, I might get to stay up late if it looks like we are working hard. On the down side, I will owe my brother a favor."
4. "I will decide tomorrow if I like this option in case the dilemma arises again." She will repeat step one to re-assess the choice she made.

Okay, I admit that this ten-year-old girl appears very self-assured, calm, and wonderfully mature. However, this child really can exist, though not always appearing this composed in the face of frustration. And, as covered in the development chapters, tens frequently blame their parents for problems, although these occurrences of misplaced blame can be exaggerated by some parents who forget how often their children *did* show and accept responsibility. If problem-solving and decision-making skills activities are used regularly in your home, this daughter could be your child more often than you realize.

*****

How a child makes decisions — or avoids them — tells us a lot about her emotional approach to life. An anxious child is likely to procrastinate in making a choice or manipulate someone else into making the decision for her. In part, the anxious child likes to please others and also fears reaching the "wrong" conclusion. Often, she knows more about what others want than what she wants for herself. Mostly, *she just wants the anxiety to go away.* Be patient but be firm in setting deadlines. Avoid accepting excuses. If you get forced into making the choice when her deadline is not met, flip a coin or roll dice, thereby leaving the final choice up to luck.

A child with ADHD is more impulsive in deciding than other children so she will tend to either decide too quickly or will not stop to make a decision at all. Such a child needs structure and guidance from you. She will not tend to hide from making her choice like the anxious child. The ADHD child requires help with steps two, three, and four. You may have to do the writing for your ADHD child to speed the activity to hold her attention.

The depressed child, sadly, backs away from choosing by withdrawing from the situation or by becoming irritable if pressed to choose. Her view is often characterized by the following outlook: "If something goes wrong, that is normal for me — somehow, I deserved it; if something goes well, that was luck — and good times do not last long for me." *Do not force choices in the face of the overwhelming stress* of misery. Use effective listening.

Effective listening required a good deal of calm talking. Decision-making required a lot of planning and commitment. Natural consequences require a minimum of talking about the problem — do not ignore him in other areas — and a commitment by the parents to not interfere with the child's problem. This exercise works very well when the repeated use of listening and problem-solving do not result in changing your child's behavior. These interventions can, of course, be used together: they are not mutually exclusive.

Natural Consequences

Life is an excellent teacher. In life, most behavior begets its own positive and negative consequences naturally. If your son plays well with others, his positive consequence is that he will be desired as a friend. If he becomes too demanding of getting his own way, the negative consequence will be that others may seldom play with him. If he completes his homework on schedule, he may be given added privileges at home and at school because he proves his responsibility to you and to his teachers. If he procrastinates in starting his homework or denies having homework when he does have some, he will have to do it when you say so or after school in the classroom since he proves he cannot handle age-appropriate responsibility well enough for his age.

These natural consequences are very effective motivators for our children (and for us) in trying to repeat their victories and to avoid repeating their mistakes. Unfortunately, many parents inadvertently negate the great effectiveness of natural consequences by taking the responsibility for their child when the problem is the child's issue. In such instances, we treat *their* appropriate displeasure as our emergency. For example, your son,

Brian, aged 12, repeatedly cannot find cannot find his favorite drawing materials because his room is an ongoing mess. You have encouraged him to keep his room neater but your suggestions fall on deaf ears. You have tried setting up a schedule according to a problem-solving sheet, although you did most of the writing and he merely sat as you worked out his solutions. Finally you clean his room for him "one more time" with your lecture that someday he will be in college and nobody will clean for him. What he has learned is either:

(1) "If I stall long enough, Mom will clean my room for me. At college, I won't have to put up with her nagging;" or

(2) "If I want to see Dad get red-faced and screaming, I just say, "I like this mess" and then I quote that sign Dad has on his desk about how a messy desk is a sign of a healthy mind.

Key hint: *when you are worrying more* about your child's ongoing negative consequences *than he is, you are overly involved* with *his* issue. It is time to step back and let the natural consequences occur. Let him cry some schoolday morning because he couldn't find the special pencils he told the teacher he would bring. And do not ruin your morning coffee break scavenging through his room to help him find the football he planned to bring for lunch recess. Don't bail him out when the problem is based upon his sloppiness due to laziness.

Similar to effective listening, natural consequences *do not apply to family issues.* If your Brian does not clean up his mess in the living room — a room that the family shares — then direct intervention is appropriate. Such intervention involves him putting away his models, books, art supplies, roller blades and, baseball card collection (especially that mint-condition Mickey Mantle rookie card worth $6,240.00) as soon as possible; or being placed in time out until he is willing to comply with your demand to put his stuff away if he balks too long. Confiscating his possessions or prohibiting him from playing in the family room for a few days may also be appropriate considering his age. (Notice that I did not recommend throwing his things away as many of us parents threaten to do after stepping barefoot on one of those roller blades.)

Deciding when and how to allow for natural consequences is based upon development and ability to learn from consequences. Prior to middle childhood, most children do not have the intellectual ability to fully connect their behavior to most of the consequences they receive. Be sure to explain these connections as soon as your child is calm enough to listen. Keep your explanations short, especially if you are providing those consequences. Your child will request more detail when he wants it and/or you can review the incident in the future. When your son is a pre-teen, especially around the age of ten, you are to blame for many problems in his eyes. The potency of natural consequences may erode significantly during this particular year. Lower your expectations for yourself and your child as necessary.

The greatest *challenge* for effective parenting — being both fair and responsible — is *knowing which parenting intervention to use and when to use it.* In general, when the problem belongs to the child alone, offer effective listening, encourage problem-solving, and then allow for natural consequences to take place. Continue to offer the problem-solving process when he complains about his problem next time. When the problem affects the family, use direct intervention *as lightly as possible* to enforce family rules. The upcoming chapters will explain these direct interventions for family issues.

*****

When repeated negative natural consequences do not result in your son's improved behavior, consider the possibility of depression wherein he may feel helpless to remedy his predicament. This sense of helplessness represents depression more than opposition or immaturity. Natural consequences are seldom effective with depressed children. *Consequences,* both positive and negative, *work best when your child feels he can either avoid the negatives or increase the positives* in the future. The future may be coming in the next year or may start tomorrow depending upon the situation.

If you are convinced that the problem is an ongoing battle of wills with your child, consider having a mediator, using contracts, using forced options (both to be explained in upcoming chapters), or getting professional help. Meeting power battles with power, especially after the onset of middle childhood, is seldom helpful — certainly not in the long run. What occurs is *an ongoing cycle of mutual stubbornness* between the two of you.

If you use natural consequences with an anxious child, be certain to combine the use of effective listening *after* the consequence has taken place. Then use problem-solving which, when anxiety is high, often works best if you do the writing and breathing is used extensively. *Stay on the subject and in the present tense.*

Due to problems with the organization of ideas, natural consequences are seldom useful with ADHD or learning disabilities where following directions is a deficit. Use problem-solving immediately after the consequence is given or the benefit is earned. *Review these written notes* with your ADHD and LD child when similar occasions are coming up. Be sure to review the earning of positive consequences just as emphatically as the negative results.

Having your child keep an About Me Book will also help. *Do not take for granted that your child knows how the consequence was earned just because there was a happy ending.*

Roundtable discussions mix effective listening and natural consequences together in a forgiving setting — home — within an often less-forgiving world. Peers, neighbors, colleagues, and school authorities, more so than parents, tend to hold grudges more while often praising less. Negative consequences are usually shorter-lived at home — a place that provides more second chances to make corrections in learning the team cooperation that roundtables are intended to build.

Roundtable Discussions

Roundtable discussions help families improve their teamwork. They build greater mutual cooperation and enthusiasm while increasing the family identity of each individual through a free exchange of ideas and shared decision-making. Roundtables are hopefully attended by all in the household. Everyone should certainly be encouraged to be present. However, do not insist upon a defiant child, most often a pre-teen, to attend the meeting or power battles will most likely result instead of the focus on the topics you had intended to discuss. Try to postpone a meeting if a child refuses to attend because of an *occasional* argument he is having with you. Do not postpone meetings if the same child is repeatedly holding out as this is then an obstinate ploy to disrupt your family agenda. And the parents should — and need to — set the the family agenda. *A home where the parents are not ultimately in charge is a chaotic and frightening place* for children — and for the parents as well. The roundtable activity is used to discuss and solve family issues and works well in healthy families. When the children or individual child holds the majority of family power, the family is, at the least, temporarily dysfunctional.

The types of roundtable topics are:

1. *Simple Topics* such as where the family will go for supper on Friday night, which movie to see together, sharing the phone, and showering schedules so everyone gets a fair share of hot water.

2. *More Complicated Topics* such as dividing family chores, when and where to do homework, sharing the family computer, sharing the best television (including holding the remote control), sharing video games, and planning a family menu for the week.

3. *Intricate Topics* including planning a vacation within a budget, setting guidelines for solving sibling arguments, and *how to break stalemates* at family roundtable discussions fairly.

Any family member can request a roundtable meeting for any family subject. Equally important, the parents must decide which subjects are open to children's actual decision-making input and which topics the children are welcome to express an opinion on only. *Children do not get any input regarding marital issues* since only the parents are in the marriage portion of the family. There are three levels of child input:

1. *Solely Parental Prerogative.* These issues cover medical appointments, school attendance, and counseling for the family. The family discussions for these topics are for covering options and opinions only. The parents make all decisions. Period. Usually children will want a discussion, hoping to get a vote. There is no vote on these topics and the children need to accept

this at the outset. Their input can only influence the parents' decision at best, however, at times, this will happen. Natural consequences do not ever apply here except in the case of a child repeatedly refusing to attend the roundtables, thereby losing a chance to offer ideas in decisions that will effect them as a family member. We cannot let our children's teeth rot or permit physical battles between children to continue unabated while waiting for them to "learn the hard way." Be certain that your children understand that the Parental Prerogative meetings are for *opinion only*. *Do not hold this type of meeting often* because the children mostly want to be in on the deciding part more than on the discussion part.

2. *Joint Parent-Child Territory.* Parents make the final decision on topics such as vacation locale, budgets for family recreation, how much to spend on home remodeling and redecorating, and bedtimes. The discussions consider opinions by all in the home, however, the parents make the final decisions. Most decisions reached here are temporary and need to be revised from year to year. Again, be certain the children understand that they are giving opinions only at this meeting.

3. *Equal Voting Topics.* Parents agree to share one-person, one-vote democratic power on issues including chore assignments, sharing the family room, and choosing family television shows. *All get to give opinions. All get an equal vote.* Use dice or a spinner to break tie votes. Parents need to be certain that they are willing to let the issues here be decided by the family team.

It is paramount for the development of family trust that once the type of decision method in the roundtable discussion is chosen that it not be arbitrarily changed by the parents after the decision is reached. For example, to deny the restaurant choice reached by equal voting because the mother or father does not like the place chosen *undermines family unity and trust and respect* for the parents. If you overrule a vote you undermine the very reason for holding the roundtable meeting. Also remember that equal voting will be the children's undisputed preference for any discussion. Decisions reached in this way may take longer since there are more people involved in the process. But they will be followed better and enthusiasm for them will usually be higher... Well, except maybe for the chores. Here are some guidelines to help insure your family's roundtable success:

1. *Choose simple subjects at first* to build family decision-making teamwork. Then go on to more complicated topics prior to tackling the really intricate and controversial issues.

2. Allow each family member up to two minutes to discuss his idea and reasons behind it. Each member is allowed a second turn if he wants to clarify his idea or ask questions about options others have brought up.

3. When agreement cannot be reached smoothly, *do not decide until another meeting.* This allows greater time for considering all options, combining ideas, or creating new ones.

4. Decide at the outset of each meeting whether the decision will be reached by vote, coin toss, taking turns, or some other *pre-agreed* method if

a consensus is not reached. Avoid forming consistent teams and voting blocks since roundtable discussions are meant to build a sense of participation in a climate of fairness. If, for example, both parents or mom-and-the girls consistently vote together, then a sense of manipulation results thereby contaminating the all-family group theme of roundtable discussions.

5. Choose a date to reevaluate the team decision when the project is ongoing, such as chore assignments. All effective decisions need to be reassessed periodically even when things are going smoothly. *Don't "quit while you're ahead."*

6. Let the children take turns running the meetings, taking notes, and being time-keeper. The more involved they are in the meetings, the more responsible they will behave at meetings and in following through on the decisions the group reaches.

Since roundtable discussions are a new concept and procedure for many families, *be patient* with the process. New activities seldom proceed smoothly at first — this is true even in the healthiest of families.

*****

If, as parents, you are unsure which decision process to use at your table, choose the Joint Parent-Child Territory and pick a simple topic. It is easier to change to the voting option at meetings than to revoke it. Otherwise, you risk setting a precedent that children always get to vote. Promise the children that the next discussion will be on a subject where they can have an equal vote. (If you already have a form of roundtables in your home, merely review the guidelines to increase success.)

Insist upon *mutual respect* for everyone's ideas and feelings. This does not mean you should hold the meeting in a deadly serious vein. To the contrary, these meetings should be enjoyable in addition to being sincere and even-handed.

By now the members of your family are talking more openly, being less contrary, and seeing you as more equitable in your regulations and the doling out of positive and negative consequences. (This does not mean, however, that your children will be saying, "Thanks for grounding me. I learned a lot during my temporary imprisonment.") Keep a journal of your improvements, efforts, achievements, and good times as parents and as a family. And when those "Thanks Mom and Dad" moments occur, you will be sure to remember them. Opening up your record book will also help those non-stop arguing and bickering days stay in perspective.

Good News Books

There is a frequent and unfortunate human tendency to remember negative experiences more readily than positive events. This may be due to our animal instinct for survival as a priority over enjoyment. Thus, we need to learn to increase our ability to hold on to the personal strengths and successes in our lives. Further, self-esteem is built upon acknowledging our victories, appreciating our efforts in our near-victories, and knowing that we can somehow handle the social, emotional, and physical dangers we face in life. To counter-balance our natural focus on fears and challenges, we need a system to retain the positive aspects of life.

For children of all ages, I suggest keeping a Good News Book to balance the perspective of life when our children get that panicky feeling that they are surrounded by physical, academic, emotional, or social doom. It involves keeping a record of successes, efforts, humilities, and hilarities. *Only each individual can define what deserves her pride* although others — especially parents — can give reminders and hints as they observe something worthy of mention.

Here is the simple approach: each person chooses a notebook of his or her own. The boundaries about the *privacy of a book's contents are paramount:* each person decides what will be shared with others and this must be mutually respected.

The Good News Book activity is best done as a family and both parents are as involved as possible. (Note that teenage children may not participate regularly and this is usually not a vital place to make a power stand with your teen.) When only one parent runs the Good News Book meetings, full credibility and effectiveness with the children is lowered — the message to the children is that complimenting ourselves and each other is not really of importance, being "only for girls," "only for young children," and so on.

There are five types of Good News Book entries:

1. *Success.* This denotes getting the results she sought at the outset of the task, *reaching the goal she set* for herself. An eight-year-old girl may be satisfied with raising her grade of C in math to a B-minus. Her eleven year-old sister may not be satisfied with having only two "boyfriends." As a caution, pursuing someone else's goal for her is codependent as it means her focus is on avoiding disapproval versus building her own identity and esteem.

2. *Effort.* Giving sincere energy to reaching goals and giving herself credit for trying helps her to prevent perfectionism or extreme competitiveness. The emphasis here is on acknowledgment of the enjoyment in the process of performing tasks. *Humility is*

frequently encountered here. Further, there is the message that we learn by trying. It is said that Thomas Edison, after making many unsuccessful gadgets, supposedly commented, "I have succeeded in learning over one thousand things *not* to do."

3. *Luck.* Having things go our way for no objective reason. We often ignore the fact that luck plays a significant part in our opportunities and successes. Every family reunion barbecue that gets good weather is proof of good luck.

4. *Whew.* Preventing trouble by a stroke of luck as in, "It could have been worse" or "Boy, was that close." When the uncle you detest cannot make it to that same family reunion, that is an example of whew.

5. *Fun.* Having a good time, especially when you had not planned anything special. These times are to be savored.

Here are some guidelines for making Good News Books effective while not having them become laborious activities. (a) List up to three items daily or close to daily as possible. (b) Resist telling your child what to write especially on an ongoing basis. Past memories are okay, too. She will think of something eventually. Again, hints and reminders of how you are and were proud of her are nice to hear. *Mention your pride in your children often;* (c) Each entry should contain enough information so that the incident can be recalled in the future. Two sentences are plenty. This is not a diary; (d) Spelling and grammar do not count; (e) Allow decorating, using cutouts from magazines, photos, ticket stubs, etc, along with, or in place of, the actual writing of information particularly if your child dislikes writing.

Further, some children prefer to work artistically instead of verbally. Up to age ten, this is an excellent family activity. Avoid setting rules or making participation a battleground.

Doing Good News Books as a family will make parenting more of a *success,* with everyone enjoying the *effort* in the long run and short run. Most of all, it will be *fun. Whew,* this chapter is over. I sure am *lucky* you bought this book.

* * * * *

Good News Books are effective with a frequently anxious child, although she may resist doing one or try to manipulate you into telling her what to write. She often does not have the confidence to set realistic expectations for her own success entries or to applaud herself for her attempts and perseverance. Focus on the entries for effort and luck.

Good News Books help to ease depression, especially with fun and luck topics. Be patient when your depressed child is dispirited or sad since she lacks the energy to believe happiness and hope exist in her own life. Do not insist she write anything.

An ADHD child responds well to success and luck entries.They help her build a balanced perspective of her life instead of over-focusing on her failures and miseries. However, you may have to do the writing for her. It is important that she have a written record since her impulsivity can result in quick esteem slides during which she cannot depend upon her memory to recall positives to restore balance to her self-image. Since ADHD is a deficit in organization, she has difficulty locating the mental list of her strengths when she needs to recall them most. Art will often be her preferred form of expression, but beware of her starting major art projects to display the equivalent of one sentence. With ADHD and learning deficits effecting graphomotor skills (physical and/or visual aspects of writing), consider using a tape or video recorder as another option.

This chapter is about a motivational and incentive activity to be used when there is a parent-child disagreement and you have decided to offer a contract. You want your child to do something that he does not want to do — and the topic is not a family issue. (You can offer a contract to your spouse too, to make his lasagna more often when it is his day to cook — or maybe to make it less often.) Although some parents do not believe in bargaining, deal making goes on in much of life. The school where I work as a counselor offers me a yearly financial agreement. The basic terms for my part-time job could be summarized as follows: If I do my job properly, I get paid the agreed-to hourly rate. If my performance is low, they will either offer me less money next year or find someone else to do the job. If my performance is good, my job is secure and I may even get a raise. Contracting involves mutual respect in the agreement process. When a contract is started, make an entry in your Good News Book under "effort." If the contract is successfully completed, make note of it under "success."

Contracts

There are times when you want your children to follow your advice or directives without your having to enforce an arbitrary rule. For example, your nine-year-old son Jack insists that he likes his room messy. No surprise here: food, rooms, and how children spend their own money are three areas that commonly *receive more parent-child arguments than necessary.* There are enough topics to argue about that really *do* deserve a strong parental stand. Your rule for Jack is "no allowance if his room not kept neat and tidy." He is broke for the fifth consecutive week. He whines about unfairness, and states "You never care about how I want my room to look!" There is no end in sight to the standoff. Jack is headstrong — much like you were at his age (and, as your spouse often claims, you still are). Like parent, like child. On the positive side of Jack's strong-willed approach to life, he is energetic and persistent in approaching the tasks he favors (like exploring the local stream, doing math, and washing cars for income) and stubborn about tasks he views as a waste of time (like cleaning his room). In addition, he is disorganized by nature and neatening his room really is tough for him. You sincerely believe that Jack needs a reward to work toward in helping him build a habit of straightening up his quarters. You tried letting him suffer the natural consequences and helped him list options for solving the problem of seldom being able to find things — all to no avail. At these times, contracts can be highly effective. Since you will need to offer rewards so he will agree with the contract you offer, you keep in mind that Jack loves professional baseball, going camping, and exploring anything outdoors.

A successful contract will be *perceived as fair by all* participants. All must fully agree to the total contract before signing. *A bad contract is worse than no contract at all.* A bad contract can cause resentment and distrust as well as ruin chances for future compromises. (A contract is an agreement to be mutually trustworthy, to sincerely seek a compromise, and not to manipulate the other person to get your way in a quick victory.) I cannot over-emphasize this attitude of both sides winning.

As with roundtable discussions, the parent decides at the outset which topics are parent prerogative and which are open for negotiation. Once you decide to solve a given issue via contract, *you are obligated* to use it as long as mutual good faith is the spirit of the talks. Of course, you can decide not to use further contracts about a particular issue and admit that a mistake was made.

Anyone can propose a topic for contract consideration and anyone can respond by "yes, no, or *I'll think about it.*"

The same is true for *any* proposal offered within the contract since there will be bargaining involved. Bargaining skills are good to have in life.

Contracts are best used as motivation for new tasks or to improve skills. Once the task can be smoothly accomplished, no further contracting about it is necessary. Here are some guidelines for successful contracting:

1. Discuss the aspects of the contract for ten minutes. If no agreement is reached, continue on another day. *Do not rush to finish* just to finish. I repeat: do not rush. Again, a bad contract is worse than no contract. Far worse.

2. If an agreement is not reached on the second day, wait two days before continuing. After that,

wait a week. Often *the mere process of talking openly and respectfully* about what is important to each other can result in greater compromise and mutual cooperation even if an formal agreement is never reached. Do not get mentally stuck on the idea that you must get a contract written, much less written right away.

3. Maintain an atmosphere of mutual respect, trust, and teamwork. The contracting process is a modified roundtable discussion for two people in which each gets an equal vote.

4. Keep the specific terms of the agreement *as simple as possible.* The more complicated the terms of the contract, the greater the chance of failure and blame later.

5. Have the duration of the contract be *as short as possible.* Rewrite it and amend it when necessary to continue motivation.

6. Have a witness sign the contract also. The role of the witness is to review the contract with both people to be sure that they fully understand all the terms of the contract. The witness does not have to agree completely with the contract specifics, but should not sign if he has serious misgivings.

Let's continue with the example of Jack who is still not keeping his room clean: something you feel is important. Jack, in age-appropriate fashion, senses an opportunity for himself and says, "I'll clean my room once a month for you, if you take me and a friend to the mall every month and give us ten bucks each to spend an anything we want."

Although Jack's offer is somewhat outlandish, he has, in effect, offered you a contractual arrangement. He is considering your concerns for a cleaner room. At this point, you can pursue one of three options. *First,* you can drop the issue (refusing the contract idea) and hope that the natural consequences of missing items eventually motivates Jack to be neater — in other words, that he matures and realizes the wisdom you have been trying to impart unto him. *Second,* you can take control (not the author's recommendation) saying, "I will vacuum once a week and I will put everything left on your floor in a box to go in the basement." *Third (and recommended),* you can consider a contract. Let's assume you wisely follow option three. In addition, you recall that Jack kept his half of deal he made with you a few months ago.

"Jack," you respond, "I will consider a written agreement with you. However, I do not accept the terms you just proposed. As a counter-offer, I would like you to keep your room reasonably uncluttered — not necessarily worthy of an award for cleanliness. For this effort I will take you to the mall at the end of each school grading period. You can have McDonald's each week and bring a friend there." This provides him with a minor payoff that occurs soon while his motivation is still strong. This arrangement also offers him a larger jackpot that he can get in a few months.

Jack, knowing he was not going to get everything he requested in the first place, adds, "Will you also take me to the Pizza Palace every other month including three bucks for the video games there?"

You nod in cautious agreement and state that the written contract will be good for one semester only, at which time you will re-negotiate and write another one *if* it is found to be mutually necessary. You also understand that the odds are close to zero that Jack will keep his room neat happily-ever-after once the contract is over. But who knows, he may get to like having things a little neater.

In parent-child relationships having less trust or low mutual respect, the process may take a few meetings.

Contracts tending to go unsigned or seldom ending with mutual satisfaction may signify deeper problems possibly requiring professional intervention.

*****

Your twelve-year-old daughter Georgia has been listening from the next room and requests a contract similar to Jack's except that she wants two friends plus fifty dollars to spend on clothing and cookies at the mall and wants you to disappear while she shops. You tell Georgia that she already keeps her bedroom neat. "However, if we need a contract to help you form better habits in the future, I will consider it," you explain in a consoling voice. In the back of your mind, you remember that Georgia's school grades were not as good as usual on the last report card...

Actually, Georgia might not want a contract because she wants to appear older and more mature than Jack. Jack's seven-year-old sister, however, would certainly like to make a deal. For her age, rewards should be made on an almost daily basis or she may at least earn daily points toward a reward that she can cash in weekly. The concept of negotiating would be simplified whereby you would limit her reward options at the outset.

In terms of mental health, contracts are seldom useful with depressed children because they expect things to go wrong and may, unconsciously, find a way to sabotage the contract. The anxious child needs a timer to limit the amount of time spent discussing the contract. A timer helps him keep all his worries to a minimum or else the contract will never get completed due to his perfectionistic distractions. Contracts with ADHD children should be kept simpler and shorter in duration. These children should have more frequent and quicker agreements in order to lessen their distractibility from the terms of your agreement.

ADHD children will also require *more reminders* for success, so plan on providing these cues instead of getting frustrated with what appears to be his forgetfulness.

The next few chapters deal with the use of punishment during the middle childhood years. You will recall that the goals of discipline are to maintain appropriate, realistic, and peaceful coexistence in your home. At times, as parents, we are like preadolescents ourselves: we can become uncertain of exactly what it is we want from our children or even from ourselves and spouses. At such times we tend to be more extreme and impulsive in using too firm a hand or be too lenient out of low energy and indecision due to our own frustration level being higher. When this being-too-harsh or being-too-tolerant becomes a pattern take your deep breaths and review your decision options to help you get out of this parenting quagmire. And remind yourself that every parent — counselors included — get caught in the parenting quicksand from time to time.

Control And Respect

Bob came to my office because his wife insisted. She felt that Bob was unnecessarily demanding of the children. "Linda says I'm too controlling, that I don't respect the kids' needs. But I say that kids need to know who is in charge. It's that way for me at work, and it's that way at school for them. They need to respect me as their father."

The sleuth inside me investigated the clue. "What do you mean by 'respect,' Bob?"

"The kids should do as I say and respect my reasons without argument. When it is time to do homework, they should do it. And when it's time to play, then play, They should listen to me, love me, and respect me."

"You seem to want a number of different things from your kids all called respect," I said. "You want them to be obedient to you, for them to build self-discipline, to be able to be playful, and to look up to you. You can have some of each of your wishes, but not if any one item is in the extreme. You are rigid in your demands yet you want the kids to be flexible enough to be playful and resourceful. If you don't model flexibility, they won't learn it. If you insist that they do things your way, then they won't learn how to make decisions for themselves. If you don't listen to them, they won't really care what you have to say — and this is the crux of respect. You *can't demand arbitrary control* over people and get their respect at the same time."

I gave Bob some handouts on listening skills and an activity to use for scheduling his children's homework (which is really about decision-making and natural consequences together). In the future, I may explain family roundtable discussions, but Bob is not ready for team decision-making yet. I encouraged Bob to keep a Good News Book for himself to cover parenting skills with a heavy emphasis on his efforts and breathing to ten.

*****

I made an appointment for Linda next since I was fairly certain she was not setting adequate limits for the kids. One parent usually *overcompensates* with leniency when the other parent is domineering. "Opposites attract" but they do not necessarily make effective problem-solving teammates.

Punishment is a form of discipline used with the intent of discouraging behavior of which we disapprove. Punishment is also used to protect our children through giving them negative consequences less harsh than than the more permanent discomforts they might possibly receive through natural consequences. It is impossible to totally avoid using punishment in raising children, nor should we try to. However, we do need to use punishment judiciously and logically.

Life offers us many punishments. Just think back to the last time you drove at twice the speed limit down a one-way street opposite the flow of construction traffic. Better to get a ticket than to suffer the more immediate and lasting consequences of a head-on meeting with the loaded dump truck rumbling toward you. Sometimes punishment is necessary as well as effective. Often, however, it is a knee-jerk response and not really the best course of action.

Punishment: When, How, and Why

Punishment is a negative consequence given purposely by an authority figure for the purpose of preventing future repetition of an unwanted and intentional behavior. *The focus is on intent.* In terms of parenting, your child is sent to his room (the punishment) by you (the authority figure) for hitting (the unwanted behavior) his younger sister, in order to, hopefully, prevent his future use of force toward her. In reality, the use of punishment often encourages your son to show his anger toward his sister in more subtle, devious, or vicious ways as well as to have your daughter cheering internally because her crocodile tears fooled you into accepting her false innocence again. Just ask Sal and

Hal Normal about being manipulated by children.

Nevertheless, there are *times when punishment is appropriate* and necessary. Reasonable rules do need to be enforced. Such rules include violating curfews, using force with others when other solutions were clearly available, placing oneself and others in needless and thoughtless jeopardy, stealing or damaging property, or purposely defying your parental request especially with the intent to embarrass you in front of others. Keep in mind, however, that punishment, especially when used as the primary form of intervention, is the least effective form of behavior management in the long run.

As with rewards, *use the lightest possible punishment* to have your child reconsider his undesirable behavior. Eight-year-old Jeff will not pick up his roller blades from near the steps. He insists he will be using them soon as his excuse to leave them in a hazardous place. The *forced choice*, the first line of punishment intervention, you offer calmly yet firmly is, "Jeffrey, (we tend to use a child's formal name when we are annoyed) you can either move your skates now or I will confiscate them for the rest of the weekend." You give him a moment to respond. He does not make a move and you appropriately, calmly yet firmly, repeat your demand while turning to take his skates. If he hustles, Jeff can get to the skates first and move them before you take them into custody.

Forced choices are helpful in encouraging children to re-think the consequences of their behavior. Forced choices are used when a problem situation is still correctable. The message to your child is: think carefully or you will lose a part of your freedom for awhile. "Or" is the main word in forced choices. They work well at all ages but are most effective between ages seven and ten. The forced choice is the least restrictive level of punishment.

The next level of restriction is grounding. Grounding is used after the infraction has been committed. Jeff's skates were left out for the third time today and you just twisted your ankle falling over them. You consider confiscating the skates for a week when he snottily retorts, "I can still ride my bike. Besides, you don't use your ankle much — you just sit around all day." (This type of mouthiness is most common between ages ten and thirteen. Similar comments from a child below age nine is a sign of intense disrespect for authority and, when done repeatedly, a significant sign of emotional or self-control problems requiring professional assistance.) Grounding is time-out by restriction to a specific room, house, or property and is appropriate for Jeff now. The goal of this punishment is to decrease, if not bring to an end, both his attitude and lack of respect for you. (If such behavior is seen in a blended family by a child of any age, both parent and stepparent need to work to extinguish the disrespectful behavior as a team. We cannot change a child's attitude, but behavior can be increased and decreased. Using insults is a behavior.) When Jeff is grounded to his room, be sure it is not a playland of video games, TV, and phone since he may be too comfortable to do much reconsidering even though he still has lost his freedom and been barred from friends.

Grounding should only be for a period of a few days at the most. Start with an hour or less. A child needs second chances to try out his judgment and handling of temptations. Further, if you ground him for two weeks then you *also imprison yourself* for that same period. If a second grounding becomes necessary because of arrogance and purposefully uncooperative behavior shortly after the first incident, add intensity to his grounding. Have him write a problem-solving plan *so that he takes responsibility* for preventing a third occurrence. This is often more effective than adding time anyway as your goal in punishing is not to inflict misery but to educate. If your child is below age ten, help him with the problem-solving process *after he works* out the first draft.

There is a social form of grounding to be used specifically for peer problems. If your child is being negatively influenced by certain peers, he should be restricted from seeing those peers until his judgment and self-control improve or until those peers are no longer seeking him. This is especially true if theft, shoplifting, vandalism, or drug or alcohol use is involved. These situations are more common in children above age twelve. If it is a first delinquency infraction for your son together with a close friend, seek solutions together with the other child's parents prior to cutting off that friendship completely. If the transgression with his friend is not serious, consider giving the group some chores to do for you with a firm promise to contact the other childrens' parents if there is ever a recurrence.

A third form of punishment is *pay-back* to those who have been harmed or injured physically or emotionally. A pay back for spray painting and defacing a neighbor's fence is to re-paint that fence prior to any return of the child's freedom. The payback includes paying for the paint. For a preadolescent, you will need to supervise, of course. For a younger middle childhooder you will have to help as well. For shoplifting, the payback starts with your child returning the pilfered products directly to the store manager and offering to make amends. Be sure the manager or *owner does not treat the incident lightly* and merely insist your child not steal again. (At least, do not have the incident treated as trivial in front of your child. Have the infraction handled with a tone of seriousness.) If vandalism occurs a second time, arrange a visit for your child with your local police juvenile officer. Call the officer ahead of time to discuss how parents and police can work best together considering your and your child's personal strengths and weaknesses.

As a hint for sticky social situations, do not use punishment in front of your child's peers unless it is absolutely unavoidable. If you do not model respect, you teach disrespect. You may send the friends home as needed. If the peers were knowingly involved with the infraction requiring punishment, consider a meeting with the other parents to decide upon a joint consequence for the group.

*****

Whenever considering punishments be sure you do your breathe-to-ten first. Foremost, remember that your response to your child is a model for appropriate behavior and respect. You may want to write out your own problem-solving sheet regarding the incident before sentencing him *especially if you are personally prone to impulsive temper.*

Punishment works best with anxious children when used sparingly. The anxious child will often offer punishments for himself that are harsher than you would have given since overly anxious children are driven to avoid your displeasure in them. The preceding comments may not be as accurate after preadolescence begins.

Punishment is seldom effective with children having ADHD and certain learning disabilities since their diminished sense of organization hinders their ability to learn by cause-and-effect relationships. Punishment is effective because the child gets time to view options, plan self-control, and review what stimulated him to act as he did. When organizing is impaired, the awareness of these skills often does not take place effectively.

Punishment seldom works with depressed children since they are in emotional misery anyway. However, when other siblings are close in age to the depressed or ADHD child, some punishments may be necessary to diffuse the siblings' feelings of unfair treatment or favoritism even though the punishment itself will have little actual preventive effect.

When can educating our children really be a form of punishment? Read on.

The Four Sentence Lecture

The title says it all. Any lecture you give your children that goes beyond four sentences is a waste of your educational breath. This is certainly true for the following reasons:

1. They already know what you have to say on the subject. That verbal essay on why they have to obey your curfew — he can recite it right along with you.

2. Kids start ignoring the salient points of our diatribes very quickly. They start thinking about whom they will call when they get ahold of the phone while looking you right in the eye as though they are paying rapt attention to your every word. Be honest: didn't you do the same to your parents once you found out if there was going to be a punishment and what the punishment was going to be?

3. Parents with a history of being long-winded are ignored as soon as they start the pointing their finger, putting their hands on their hips, and speak with that tone that means, "How many times do I have to tell you...?!!"

If your lecture is really meant to teach your child a lesson, keep it short. He will actually listen more often. To get him to be more responsible, have him write a problem-solving plan so *he takes the responsibility* for his behavior — ie, let him do some of the worrying about keeping his curfew. Have him write a horror story with a title like, "Oh, How I Wish I'd Been Home on Time." However, if your lecture is meant to be a punishment under the guise of, "I sat and worried for an hour. Now you can listen to me rant and rave for an hour," then say so at the outset. (Don't really blabber for a full hour or he will never forgive you.) Better, tape record your lecture while you are building up steam. When you catch him, give him the tape instead of the lecture. Let him listen to it in his room... Then give him a quiz. He will probably have to listen to the tape all over again to get the correct answers. After he passes the quiz, you can finally tell him what the punishment will be, that is, if he has not suffered enough already. Reminder: don't really yap for a whole sixty minutes.

*****

Remember, when you are angry, keep your important points to a few select sentences. *Four or less.* Good luck.

Before you punish your daughter consider her point of view and the factors she believes influenced her behavior and decisions. This does not mean you are accepting her excuses, it just signifies that you are listening to better understand how she envisions the situation. Doing this may not necessarily alter the consequences you had initially planned — although that could certainly happen at times. Mostly, it may alter how you present your intervention to her including an explanation of your reasons behind your disciplinary action or postponement of it. Almost every situation has two or more viewpoints, with some validity on each side. The same is true for misunderstandings.

Mutual Blame

They sat in my office, both gritting their teeth and breathing shallow, angry breaths. I looked at twelve-year-old Zach first. "I assume that both of you are telling the truth as you see it," I began. "My goal is not to find who, or if anyone, is at fault since that seldom does much good in family disagreements."

The mother could not wait. "Zach does not help with chores, he is disrespectful to his stepfather and me, and his report card stinks! Zach says he does not like our new house and he wants to move back to the old, cramped, place we had before I changed jobs. Both he and his sister agreed that getting a new house was worth my working extra hours and having Mitch work over-time to cover the increased mortgage."

I spoke next. "We all try to predict what life will be like after a change like moving, having our parents less available, having to make new friends, and so on. Regretting some aspects of any change is normal even if we approved of that change or even initiated it...Zach, how do you see things?"

There were tears in Zach's eyes and indignation in his voice. "Mom and Mitch said we would have less money for fun stuff if we moved to a bigger house. We moved a year ago and we never do anything because they save every cent. That's not a budget, that's prison!"

I jumped in before Zach's mother could respond defensively. "As in a stressful marriage or job, everyone feels like they were deceived by the other one. Zach, you feel that your Mom and Mitch lied about how life would be. Mom, you feel that Zach lied to you about his accepting the stringent family budget.

"Your problem is not money and lifestyle," I continued. *The problem is unresolved mutual blame.* Instead of talking about your frustrations and sharing your hopes — together with the need to modify your goals and expectations — you mutually alienate your previous pal with blame. Try to understand each other more. Neither intended to trick the other one."

I gave them some activities on effective listening, breathing to ten, and roundtable discussions. I encouraged Zach's mom to discuss family finance decisions from a parental prerogative stance with Zach and his older sister. As it stood now, the parents were making all the decisions in private — in a sincere attempt to protect the children from worrying about money matters — while the kids became disgruntled outsiders to family choices.

When in doubt, talk it out. Discussing family issues with your children does not necessarily mean you are giving them a vote, however, their participation involves them in the decision-making process and prevents mistrust. The openness greatly lessens alienation and emotional distance while doing wonders in curing mutual blame.

*****

Often, when there is mutual blame, effective listening and family roundtable discussions help everyone to see other people's validities. Further, such communication interventions lessen your parental burden. You do not have to make *all* the decisions or take full responsibility for the family's well-being. Usually when decisions and information are shared in accordance with each family member's developmental understanding and maturity, *more responsibility* is taken by the children. Parents do *less nagging.* And better still, increased caring and humility are felt by all.

Closing Thoughts

Middle Childhood is a compilation of over twenty-three years of professional experience and fifteen years of parenting. It reflects these aspects of my life — in addition to the fact that I was a child myself once upon a time (although my children somedays seem to doubt that I was ever a child, much less that I was ever a teenager). Both my childhood and my parenthood have had high points and low times. All in all, I enjoyed most of these passages. Through these eras I became more patient and confident, building greater humility and feeling increased compassion toward my children, my parents, my wife, and myself.

Hopefully, *Middle Childhood* will have a similar effect on you. The Normals illustrated how increased parenting teamwork smooths parenting and marriage at the same time. Caroline and her parents learned about themselves in order to lessen the family deficits of the prior generation while keeping the strengths and love that their parents also handed down. The developmental knowledge you gained in *Middle Childhood* will help you to avoid unnecessary battles while encouraging you to better motivate and structure your children. The section on discipline should help you balance and assess your style of providing *positive and negative* consequences for your children and your family.

What to do next? Go back to the beginning, and as the first section's title says, *Get Started.* Enjoy being a parent. Overcome the desire to put other tasks ahead of the time you can otherwise spend with your children. Improvement of your parenting, not perfection, is the goal. Take small steps in increasing your style and skills and you will go far. Best of luck. *You can do it.*

Bibliography

(* Denotes helpful reading for general parenting as opposed to professional texts used in preparing Middle Childhood.)

American Psychiatric Association. *Diagnostic and Statistical Manual of Mental Disorders.* 4th edition. Washington, DC : American Psychiatric Association, 1994.

* Ames, Louise Bates, Frances Illg, and Sidney M. Baker. *Your Ten to Fourteen-Year-Old.* New York: Dell Publishing Co., 1998.

* Bach, George R. and Ronald Deutach. *Stop! You're Driving Me Crazy.* New York : Berkley Books, 1979.

Beavers, Robert W. *Successful Marriage: A Family Systems Approach to Couples Therapy.* New York : W. W. Norton, 1985.

Benjamin S. Bloom, editor. *Developing Talent in Young People.* New York : Ballantine Books, 1985.

* Brazelton, T. Berry. *Touchpoints : Your Child's Emotional and Behavioral Development.* Reading, Mass : Addison-Wesley, 1992.

* Canter, Lee. and Lee Hausner. *Homework Without Tears.* New York : Harper & Row., 1987.

* Covey, Stephen R., Roger Merrill and Rebecca Merrill. *First Things First.* New York : Simon & Schuster, 1994.

* Dodson, Fitzhugh. *How to Father.* Los Angeles : New American Library, 1974.

* Dreikurs, Rudolph and Vicki Soltz. *Children: the Challenge.* New York: Hawthorne Books, Inc., 1964.

* Fadem, Susan S. *Parenting in the 90's.* St. Louis, MO : Virginia Publishing Co, 1992.

* Fluegelman, Andrew. *The New Games Book.* Garden City, N.J. : Doubleday & Co. Inc., 1976.

* Fraiberg, Selma H. *The Magic Years.* New York : Charles Scribner's Sons, 1959.

* Friends in Recovery. *The Twelve Steps for Adult Children from Addictive Families.* San Diego : Recovery Publications, 1989.

Group for the Advancement of Psychiatry. *The Joys and Sorrows of Parenthood.* New York : Charles Scribner's Sons, 1973.

* Hallowell, Edward and John Ratey. *Driven to Distraction.* NewYork : Simon & Schuster, 1994.

* Heldmann, Mary L. *When Words Hurt.* New York : Ballentine Books. 1988.

Kastenbaum, Robert. *The Psychology of Death.* 2nd ed. New York : Springer Publishing Co., 1992.

* Kushner, Harold S. *When All You've Ever Wanted Isn't Enough.*
New York : Pocket Books, 1986.

* Kushner, Harold S. *When Bad Things Happen to Good People.* New York : Avon Books, 1981.

Levine, Mel. *Educational Care.* Cambridge, Mass : Educators Publishing Service, 1994.

* Madaras, Lynda and Dane Saavedra. *What's Happening to My Body? A Growing Up Guide for Mothers and Daughters.* New York : Newmarket Press, 1983.

* Madaras, Lynda and Dane Saavedra. *What's Happening to My Body? A Growing Up Guide for Parents and Sons.* New York : Newmarket Press, 1984.

Madow, Leo. Anger: *How to Recognize and Cope with It.* New York : Charles Scribner's Sons, 1972.

Nichols, Michael. *The Self in the System.* New York : Brunner/Mazel Publishers, 1987.

Robinson, Edward, Joseph Rotter, Mary Ann Fey, and Kenneth Vogel. *Helping Children Cope with Fears and Stress.* Ann Arbor : ERIC Counseling and Personnel Services Clearinghouse, 1992.

* Scarf, Maggie. *Intimate Partners.* New York : Ballentine Books, 1987.

* Spock, Benjamin and Michael Rothenberg. *Dr Spock's Baby and Child Care.* New York : Pocket Books, 1985.

* Steinberg, Lawrence and Ann Levine. *You and Your Adolescent.* New York : Harper Perennial, 1990.

Steinglass, Peter. *The Alcoholic Family.* New York : Basic Books,1987.

* Subby, Robert. *Healing the Family Within.* Deerfield Beach. Fla : Health Communications, Inc, 1990.

* Unell, Barabara and Jerry Wyckoff. *20 Teachable Virtues.* New York : Pedigree Books, 1995.

* Weinhaus, Evonne and Karen Friedman. *Stop Struggling with Your Teen.* New York : Penguin Books, 1988.

* Weinhaus, Evonne and Karen Friedman. *Stop Struggling with Your Child.* New York : Perennial Books, 1991.

Whitfield, Charles. *Healing the Child Within.* Deerfield Beach, Fla : Health Communications, Inc., 1987.

* Walker, Ellen. *Growing Up with My Children.* Center City, Minn : Hazeldon Foundation, 1988.

INDEX

208